BUILDING A WINNING PERSONALITY

RASHID MERCHANT

EMBASSY BOOKS
www.embassybooks.in

Building a Winning Personality

This edition first published in 2018

Published in India by:
Embassy Book Distributors
120, Great Western Building,
Maharashtra Chamber of Commerce Lane,
Fort, Mumbai - 400 023.
Tel : (91-22) 22819546 / 22818567.
Email : info@embassybooks.in
Website : www.embassybooks.in

Distribution Centres:
Mumbai, Bangalore, Kolkata, Chennai,
Hyderabad, New Delhi, Pune

ISBN: 978-93-88247-03-0

Page Design and Layout by PSV Kumarasamy

Dedication

I dedicate this book to Roshanara, my best friend and ever-loving wife in appreciation of and gratitude for all that she has been doing for me for the last 48 years.

To Altaf my lovable son, who has been an eternal source of infinite joy and happiness to me for the last 45 years.

Acknowledgement

I profusely thank my good friend Rukmini for all the help rendered unstintingly to enable me to create this book.

My thanks to Shri Dilip Jadhav, Librarian, Anjuman College of Hotel Management, Mumbai for the active interest he showed and the help he gave me in getting this book published.

Many thanks to Shri Santosh Kokane, proprietor, Vakratund Book House for the help and guidance given by him in making this book a reality.

Foreword

Dear reader,

With utmost humility, I present to you, a lifetime of learning in this book. I have tried to put together what I have gleaned from countless books, people, workshops, training programmes, relationships, and life. While I have tried to give credit to others wherever I have used a quotation in this book, I must acknowledge that there may be several ideas contained here that have come to me from someone else.

What has emerged as a book here is what I have internalised from hundreds of people I have interacted with, read or learnt from directly or indirectly. I learnt, and then I lived the learning. And when you grow to be 78, you have enough time to become one with the learning. So, a lot of what you are about to read may come through me, but not necessarily from me. I take this opportunity to acknowledge all those that I have learnt from. If I have not given you credit explicitly, it is only because what I have learnt from you has been woven seamlessly into the tapestry of learnings from everywhere else, to create who I am today.

I am grateful to everyone I have interacted with and everything I have read or heard or seen, for you have collectively birthed this book with me. I am but the medium of communication.

Yours truly,
Rashid Merchant

Table of Contents

Chapter 1

PORTRAIT AND PHILOSOPHY OF A WINNER

Muriel James and Dorothy Jongeward in their book "Born to win" say that a "Winner" is "One who - responds authentically by being credible, trustworthy, responsive and genuine, both as an individual and as a member of Society". To a winner, Success is "the Progressive realization of useful, worthwhile, productive and pre-determined goals he has set for himself. A winner is "Genuine". And, he is busy winning and not wasting precious time engaged in defeating others.

All successful people, all over the world, have the same lifestyle. So also, all losers. It is said that if you want to taste success, go and touch failure. The reverse is also true. What this means is that Winners have certain common qualities/ characteristics/attitudes and philosophy towards Life and Life's situations.

We will now set out these qualities: -

1. A winner regards himself as the master of his fate, the captain of his ship, the maker of his fortune, the creator of his destiny. In other words, he assumes total responsibility for his life.
2. A winner regards "Luck" as the meeting point of

opportunity and his preparation and he believes that the harder and smarter he works, the "Luckier" he gets.

3. A winner believes and knows that whatever the mind can conceive it can achieve. The human mind has amazing power. There are no limits. The only limits are those which are self-imposed.
4. A winner has a very positive attitude to "Failure". He believes that:
   a. There is no such thing as permanent failure and that every failure contains within itself the seeds of equal opportunity and success. Failure is only final when one gives up.
   b. A failure is an event, not a person.
   c. You've not failed — your plan /strategy has failed.
   d. Failure is feedback.
   e. Failure is a very good Teacher — it tells you what does not work.
   f. Failure is a stepping stone to success.
5. A winner gives results, not excuses.
6. A Winner never quits, and a quitter never wins. A winner is very persistent. He does not give up. Edison, Lincoln to mention only a couple of persons personify this trait. He persists until he succeeds. He displays the quality of "WITTS" — i.e. "Whatever It Takes to Succeed."
7. A winner knows that there is no such thing as something for nothing. In life there are no Free Lunches — to get something, you have to give something.
8. A Winner 'Goes the Extra-Mile' [G.E.M]. He does more than what he is paid for, more than what he is expected to do. A. Lincoln said, "if a man works only as much as what he is paid for, he remains a slave".

He becomes free only when he does something extra. The advantages of G.E.M are that you sharpen your ability; you gain self-respect, you get more knowledge; people, including superiors, respect you more. You gain more confidence, etc. Eventually, you are richly compensated and rewarded.

9. A Winner is decisive. He is not afraid of taking decisions in all areas of his life ¬¬¬- career, relationships, life-partner, etc. — He knows that even a wrong decision is better than no decision.
10. A Winner breaks the monotony of dull routine. He breaks free from traditional, conventional thinking.
11. A Winner knows he, like everyone else, is a unique person. He maintains his individuality. He does not "imitate' others. He follows his own 'inner urge'. He may have a role model, but he does not copy anyone. The world values the original. It has no value for Xerox Copies.
12. A Winner rises above criticism. He welcomes it, learns from it and moves on.
13. A Winner breaks the bonds/barriers of psychological slavery such as:
    a. What will people say/think of me? This is the most destructive thought. It prevents you from achieving what you want to and what you can achieve.
    b. **It's too late:** A winner does not buy this. He knows that at any age he can do what he sets his mind to do.
    c. **Security:** A Winner breaks free from his comfort zones which stifles the greatest talent. He dares to take risks. He knows that there really is no security. Life is a gamble. Or as Helen Kellar said, "Life is a daring adventure."
    d. **Past Mistakes:** A Winner is not caught up in the

grip of past mistakes. He learns from the past, plans for the future but lives in the present. He believes that:

"Yesterday is History"
"Tomorrow is a Mystery"
"Today is a Gift, that is why they call it The Present"

And

"Yesterday is a cancelled cheque"
"Tomorrow is a Promissory Note"
"Today is ready cash"

And he uses it to the hilt.

14. **A Winner is goal-directed:** He fixes the right goals and develops definite plans of action.
15. **A Winner is Self-motivated:** His motivation is not induced by Fear or Incentive. It springs from within himself and is independent of outside circumstances.
16. **A Winner has a healthy self-image:** He knows that people fail in the mind before they fail in the outside world and that every success is created twice — first in mind and then in the outside world. A Winner's healthy self-image makes him believe that he absolutely deserves success.
17. **A Winner has a Positive, Mental Attitude:** He knows that attitudes harden before arteries harden. A Winner does not whimper. He counts his blessings, not his problems. He looks at the bright side of things. He looks for the "pony" in everything.
18. **Time Management:** Time is the stuff that Life is made up of. If you waste Time, you waste Life. A Winner, therefore, manages his time very well. He identifies his Time Wasters and eliminates them. He focuses his attention and time on the highest payoff activities.

19. **Effective Speaking and Communication:** The man who can speak effectively is given far more credit than he deserves. The Top Bosses are the ones who have higher sharpness in communication. A Winner, therefore, hones his skills of effective speaking and communication.
20. **Health:** A Winner knows that if Health is lost, everything is lost. A Winner, therefore, maintains his health by following a regimen of proper diet, regular exercises and relaxation techniques to manage stress.
21. **Assertiveness:** A Winner is neither passive nor aggressive. He is an assertive person. He is able to talk to people freely, openly, directly, honestly, appropriately, and in harmony with his self-esteem without feeling guilty or emotional. He thereby ensures that life starts working for him.
22. **Human Relations:** A Winner maintains excellent relations with people around him. He practices the golden principles of good human relations with all the people he meets during the course of his life and career.
23. **Energy & Enthusiasm:** A Winner has abundant energy and enthusiasm for Life. Enthusiasm is the elixir, the spirit of his life. A Winner is excited about things. He gives everything he has got to everything he does.
24. **Practical Application:** A Winner learns what he can and uses what he learns to reap the rewards and change his life.
25. **Affirmations:** A Winner is very careful about his self-talk. He avoids all negative self-talk. He constantly feeds his sub-conscious mind with positive messages for he knows that what you say to yourself makes a huge difference.

26. **Visualization:** A Winner practices visualization. He first pictures what he wants and then actualizes it.
27. **Clarity:** A Winner is very clear about his goals. The essence of clarity is knowing where you are and where you want to go. A Winner has this clarity.
28. **Competence:** A Winner is very competent in his chosen profession. He is as good as or better than his competitors.
29. **Common Sense:** A Winner has robust common sense. Common sense is practical wisdom. It is the ability to see things as they are and deal with them as they ought to be dealt with, without being bound by text-book approaches or pre-conceived ideas.
30. **Consistency:** A Winner is very consistent about his success. He keeps on upgrading his skills and innovating to keep competitors at bay. He constantly adapts to changing conditions and learns to face new challenges.
31. **Creativity:** A Winner develops the ability to think out-of-the-box. He looks at things with new eyes and from new angles. A Winner is not imprisoned by past methods and practices.
32. **Commitment:** A Winner is 100% dedicated, committed to his cause, his country, his profession.
33. **Consideration:** He has consideration for others. He shows respect and "listens" to them attentively.
34. **Courage:** A Winner has the ability to take risks. Courage is not the absence of fear but the ability to go ahead, to decide, to take risks in spite of fear.
35. **Confidence:** Self-Confidence is the essence of a winner's personality. Confidence is not a sense of superiority or boastful arrogance. It is a calm inner self-assurance that he can deal with any situation that may arise.

Let us end this chapter by delineating the main difference between a **Winner** and a **Loser**: -

- The Winner is always a part of the Solution;
  The Loser is always a part of the problem.
- The Winner sees an opportunity in every problem;
  The Loser sees a problem in every opportunity.
- The Winner says, "It may be difficult, but it is possible";
  The Loser says, "It may be possible, but it is difficult".
- The Winner makes it happen;
  The Loser lets it happen.
- The Winner says, "Let me do it for you";
  The Loser says, "That is not my job".
- The Winner always has a program;
  The Loser always has an excuse.
- The Winner says, "I must do something";
  The Loser says, "Something must be done".

Chapter 2

Unlock Your Potential and Become a Winner

We are all born with vast potential. All of us live well within our potential. We utilize only a wee bit of our potential. It is said that even outstanding achievers such as Mahatma Gandhi, Albert Einstein, etc. have actualized only about 10-15 % of their potential. All of us have the inborn capacity, the potential, to achieve more than what we actually achieve or accomplish. Therefore, say 'yes' to your potential and become all that you are capable of becoming. As good as you are, there is still room for improvement. In fact, the biggest room in the world is the room for improvement. So, utilize your potential and become the best that you can become.

The following steps are helpful to unlock our potential:

Outgrow your self-imposed limitation

We are born to win, but we have been conditioned to lose. When we were young, we were very easily conditioned — by our parents, teachers, elders, society, etc. We received a lot of negative inputs from the environment, with the result that we have placed severe limitations on ourselves. These limitations are self-imposed.

Think of the big circus elephant who is tied with a small

chain. The elephant has the strength to easily break the chain and become free. But it has conditioned itself to believe that it cannot break free. Therefore, it does not even try.

Something similar has happened to us. We have a natural talent and ability to achieve a lot, but we have mentally handicapped ourselves. Therefore, the first step to unlock your potential is to outgrow your self-imposed limitations.

Feed better messages to your mind

The human mind is the most competent computer. It has an infinite capacity to store data. It is, therefore, most essential that you feed the correct data into your computer — your subconscious. Others may say anything, give any information. But only you can make the 'entry' into your computer. You are completely responsible for the 'data' you have stored in your 'computer'. If you feed 'bad' or 'incorrect' data to your subconscious, such as 'I am lazy; I am no good', that is what you will become. GIGO (Garbage In, Garbage out). On the other hand, if you make 'good' entries, feed 'correct' data to your subconscious, such as 'I am strong' I am energetic; I am creative', that is what you will become. You will get the desired outcome. GIGO (Good Input, Good Output). Therefore, to unlock your potential, it is imperative that you get better-operating thoughts in your subconscious.

Develop a positive, healthy attitude

Attitudes are more important than facts. Attitudes control our performances. It is your attitude, not your aptitude, which will determine your altitude. Most people have not risen to their highest potential not because of lack of skill, knowledge or opportunity, but because of their attitudes. We have developed an attitude of non-belief in ourselves. It is important to look at our limiting attitudes and work at developing the opposites (for example, converting procrastination into dynamic action).

Mind your self-talk

We are constantly talking to ourselves and what we say to ourselves makes an immense difference. Our attitude is formed by our words. Words conjure up pictures/images and what you conjure up/visualize is what will actually happen. For example, if you say to yourself, "I know I am going to fail/ forget", you sow the seeds of that event happening. Reality then follows and what you visualize is what will actually happen. Whatever you speak is what happens. What you say is what you get. Always say what you want. Most people say the things they do not want more often than they say the things they want. Always say what you want.

Your words are your tools. They predict and perpetuate your action/performance. Your subconscious is a non-judgmental computer — it merely accepts the data you feed into it and throws out the result. A hammer is a tool. You can use it to hit nails or hit your own thumb. Likewise, words are your tools. You can use them to 'unlock' your potential or to impose limitations on yourself. Learn to use your tools appropriately. Control and direct your self-talk to achieve your goals and actualize your potential.

Improve your self-image

We all have our own self-image. We work and live within it. It controls our income, status, performance, social prestige, etc. We act like the person we think we are. It is impossible to act otherwise. To unlock your potential, you have to change the inside image. This is essential. Learn to see yourself the way you want to be. Remember that it is not what you are that holds you back — it is what you think you are not, that holds you back. A potent force in unlocking your potential is to 'picture in your mind, the world you want to see'. Therefore, improve your self-image/self-esteem, so that, you believe, genuinely believe, deep down within you, that you absolutely deserve wealth, prosperity, abundance, happiness, success, rich interpersonal relationships, etc.

Accept 100 % responsibility

This is very important for unlocking your potential. Take responsibility for everything in your life. For example, if things are not going well in the office, family, neighbourhood, don't blame others; take up the responsibility to improve the situation yourself. You are not a puppet in the hands of others. Your life is not a wooden plank floating in the river. It is a ship with a rudder. You are the captain of your ship. So, take charge of your life. Do things on a 'choose to', 'want to' basis. Be accountable. Be responsible. This is a winner's lifestyle. Doing things on a 'have to', 'should do' basis is a loser's lifestyle. The more things you do on a 'want to' or 'choose to' basis, the faster you will unlock your potential. You don't have to accept life as it comes to you. Design it so that life comes to you the way you want it.

Set goals

Without goals, you leave success to chance. The strongest force in human motivation is setting goals —they give you meaning, purpose and direction. Setting goals helps you to lift the lid on yourself—to unlock your potential. In setting goals, be sure to balance and prioritise them. Most importantly, always state your goals in positive terms (what you want) and write down your goals and develop a plan of action. That will give you focus. It is important to write your goals. Writing clarifies and crystallizes your thoughts. Written goals serve as a constant reminder. Our goals are not out of reach; often, they are out of sight. Therefore, write them down, look at them daily and take appropriate action. Finally, it is desirable to dream big in positive terms; aim too high and miss; don't aim low and hit, for if you don't have a dream, how can you make a dream come true?

Ask the right questions

In any situation, asking the right questions will help you to release your potential. For example, instead of asking, "Why am I obese or overweight?" ask "What can I do to become slim and trim?" When faced with a business loss, instead of asking "Why did this happen to me?" or "Why am I so unlucky?" ask "What benefit can I derive from this?" or "How can I turn this to my advantage?" or "What lesson can I learn from this?"

Don't ask "What is wrong with me?" Instead, ask "What can I do to remedy the situation?" Once the right, empowering questions are asked, creativity is released, and the mind throws up innovative answers and solutions.

Use what you learn

Keep an open mind. Learn what you can and use what you learn to change your life. We all know a lot. We have learned a lot, but we don't practice what we know. The biggest gap is the gap between knowledge and action. Knowing is only knowing. Knowing is not doing. Doing is doing. Knowledge is only potential power. Action is real power. An ounce of practice is better than a pound of knowledge. The world rewards you for what you do and not for what you know. Thus, to unlock your potential, put your knowledge into practice — use what you know.

Practice affirmation and visualization

Affirmation is stating positively, emphatically and with

emotion, what you want to be or have, as if it is already so. Repeated affirmations help to make it a reality.

Visualization

Get a clear mental picture of what you want, fill it with emotion and hold on. Look at the picture every morning and night. In other words, see what you want and get what you see!

Inner desire/motivation to be better

One of the main reasons why we do not rise to our potential is that we think and feel that we are OK. We are satisfied with being good and good is the enemy of the best. This lack of inner desire/motivation prevents us from becoming what we are capable of becoming.

In conclusion, we may say that we are all capable of becoming much, much better than what we actually are. We are not in competition with others. We are in competition with ourselves — trying to grow and be the best that we are capable of becoming. And whether you think you can or think you can't, you are right. So, let us grow and become the best that we are capable of becoming, always remembering that success is a journey, not a destination, and that the road to success is always under construction. Also remember, that success, like Coca-Cola, comes in 'Cans' not 'Cannots'.

Chapter 3

POSITIVE MENTAL ATTITUDE [P.M.A]

Attitude can be defined as a persistent tendency to feel and behave in a particular way.

There is a well-known story of a man in the U.S.A who was selling balloons. He had a stock of balloons of various colours — Blue, Green, Yellow, Pink, Black, White, etc. When business was a little dull, to attract the attention of children, he would fill gas in the balloons and release them. The Balloons would soar high up. Once when he was releasing balloons, he felt somebody tugging at his shirt to get his attention. He looked down and saw a small African American boy who was pulling at his shirt. The black boy asked him: "Balloon man, Balloon man, if you release a black balloon, will it also fly high like the other colourful balloons"? The wise balloon man did not utter a word. He simply filled gas into the black balloon and released it. The black balloon flew high up in the air — as high as the other balloons. Then the wise man turned to the boy and said, "Young man, it is not the colour of the Balloon that makes it go up, it is what is inside the balloon that makes it fly high". And what is inside us is our Attitude. And it is our Attitude and not our Aptitude that determines our Altitude.

Your attitude is your outlook towards Life. It can be positive or negative. P.A. means having an attitude where you see the brighter side in every situation. Your attitude is a mindset. It is the way you look at things mentally. Facts are not so important. Attitude is most important. If you decide to be unhappy, you can give 100 reasons for being unhappy. Decide to be happy and you can think up 100 reasons to be happy. It is the case of looking at a glass as half full or half empty. In both cases, you are right.

Two well-qualified and equally capable salesmen were employed by a shoe company. The first salesman was sent to a remote place to promote sales of his company's shoes. On reaching there and surveying the entire town, he noticed that nobody in the town was wearing footwear. He immediately sent a wire to headquarters stating that "Nobody wears shoes. Hence, no market for our products. Am coming back". The management was not satisfied with this. They sent the 2nd salesman to the same town. He experienced the same facts. He also sent a wire to headquarters. But the content was poles apart. In his wire, he stated, "Nobody here wears shoes. Immense scope for our product. No competition also. Please ship all the shoes that the company has. Will be able to sell all of them". Same facts, totally opposite response.

Another Story: Anthony Robbins tells us about a man who had two sons. The father was an abject failure. He was an alcoholic, a drug addict and a criminal to boot, who spent the last years of his life in prison. The elder son went the way of his father and was a total failure. The younger son became highly successful in life and was very well respected in society. In an interview, when the elder son was asked the cause of his dismal life, he replied: "With a father like this, what else could I have become". When the younger son was asked how he became so successful in life, he replied: "With a father like this, what else could I have become". Again, the same facts with different outcomes.

William James of Harvard University says, "The greatest discovery of my generation is that human beings can alter their lives by altering their attitudes of mind" The foundation of success is an attitude. Shiv Khera mentions a Harvard University study which concluded that “when people get jobs, 85% of the time it is because of their attitude and only 15% of the time because of how smart they are and how many facts and figures they know”. Top executives of leading companies were asked, “what is the one thing you would like to see changed in your employees?” Without exception their response was “Better Attitude”.

Attitude is your mental focus on the outside world. In simple words, you take a picture of the life you want to take. It is wise to look at the world as if you have powerful Binoculars — make it a point to view the positive things through the magnifying end and reverse them when you face negative aspects or elements.

A P.M.A. is the outward manifestation of a mind that dwells primarily on positive matters. It is a mindset tipped in favour of creative activity rather than boredom; joy over sadness; hope over despair. A P.M.A. is the one which focuses on opportunities and not problems; on strengths and not weaknesses; on capabilities and not limitations; on powers and not difficulties; on how things can be done and not why they cannot be done. A person with a P.M.A. is aware of his weaknesses but his focus is on his strengths whereas, a person with a negative attitude may be aware of his strengths but his focus is on his weaknesses. A P.M.A. is very helpful because it triggers enthusiasm; it enhances creativity and generates higher energy levels all of which lead to greater success. According to Mattie D Babcock “One of the most common mistakes and one of the costliest is thinking that success is due to some genius, some magic, something or the other which we do not possess”. The truth is success is often the result of your attitude which is within your control. How much success you achieve in life is determined more by how you think than by any other factor in your life. A positive attitude, by itself, is no guarantee of success but it certainly enhances your chances of success. On the other hand, a negative attitude will certainly kill, or at least reduce, all chances of success.

Your attitude is influenced and shaped by your environment, education and experience. However, your attitude is not static. It is not something with which you are stuck. You can overcome your habits of bad or negative thinking and cultivate a better attitude. The following guidelines or principles will help you develop a P.M.A:

1. **Behave like a positive person:** Act like a positive person. Walk, talk, think and dress like a radiant, confident, poised and successful person. See yourself succeeding. Attitude follows action. Positive action leads to positive thoughts. When you see and think of yourself as a successful person and act like a successful person, you start to become successful. To quote Andrew Carnegie "The man who acquires the ability to take full possession of his own mind may take possession of anything else to which he is justly entitled".
2. **Look for the Positive in every situation:** We generally find what we look for. A story: Researchers kept two boys under observation in 2 different rooms. The first boy was kept in a room full of wonderful toys. The second boy was kept in a room full of horse manure. After some time, they visited the first boy expecting him to be enjoying himself thoroughly with the lovely toys. They were surprised to see him glum and complaining and moaning about the colour of the toys, the shape and size of the toys, etc. Then they went to the 2nd boy expecting him to be dull and dejected. To their surprise, they found the 2nd boy playing gleefully and enthusiastically with the horse manure. When queried about this, he replied: "With so much horse manure in the room, I was sure that there would be a pony somewhere near". The moral is

"Look for the Pony in every situation. Be Optimistic. Look for the brighter side of things".

3. **Develop a sense of Humour:** The one factor that separates a person with a positive attitude from the person with a negative attitude is a Sense of Humour. The more you develop a sense of humour, the more positive you will become and vice-versa.
4. **Develop the habit of taking prompt action:** Don't put off doing things. Putting off things tires you and leads to negativity. Take immediate action. Adopt the T.N.T formula, i.e. Today, Not Tomorrow.
5. **Count your Blessings:** Focus on the things that you have and be grateful for them. Develop the habit of gratitude. We have a lot to be grateful for. Take your mind off the things that you don't have.
6. **Simplify your Life:** Remove clutters from your life. Get rid of unused and unappreciated possessions and goods that you don't need or have time to enjoy. Don't over-extend yourself. Do not get involved in too many activities. It will hassle you and take a heavy toll on your attitude. Also, don't put off attending to little things like small health problems, minor repair jobs, etc. Such problems do not vanish. In the course of time, they become major problems which then adversely affect and impact your attitude. It is also important to maintain a healthy balance between career and home. Lastly, it is imperative to shed worn-out relationships. Holding on to negative/meaningless relationships majorly affects your attitude. You must learn to let go of such relationships in order to protect your Attitude. However, simplifying is not easy. It takes efforts to simplify. But simplify you must. Remember, it is simple to be happy, but it is difficult to be simple.
7. **Shed or get rid of the Negatives in your life:** Avoid

negative people who tend to pull you down. Always try to be in the company of successful people — the achievers. Their influence will have a beneficial effect on you — it will pull you up. Likewise, avoid movies and T.V programs which contain violence and other forms of negativities. Similarly, be very particular about the newspapers and books that you read. Read material which uplifts you and strengthens you mentally.

8. **Make a good beginning at the start of everyday:** Remember that every day is the first day of the rest of your Life. Begin everyday enthusiastically and in a positive manner. Make positive affirmations as soon as you wake up. Spend the first hour of the day soaking yourself with positive and inspirational thoughts. Read motivational books or listen to motivational tapes

9. **Insulate:** In spite of your best efforts, it may not be possible for you to eliminate all the negative influences and factors in your life. There may remain a few no-win situations for e.g., a permanent physical disability; an intractable family problem, etc. You have to learn to accept them and live with them and manage to stay positive. People have managed to stay positive in spite of such problems. You need to apply techniques so that these negatives do not affect or impact on your attitude. In other words, insulate your focus against the negative factors. Some of the things you could do are:

    a. Adopt the "One-day-at-a-time" Philosophy. Live in the present

    b. Use Humour

    c. Keep Busy

    d. Engage in vigorous exercises

e. Do something for others
f. Concentrate on positive thoughts
g. Talk it out
h. Spend time with a good friend
i. If you believe in God, hand over your problems to God
j. Laugh it out
k. If possible, move into a different environment.

10. **Improve your Appearance:** When you improve your appearance, you give your P.A. a boost. When you look good, it enhances your self-image and the world seems brighter. It also helps you to be more in focus. The connection between a good self-image and a P.A. is real and vital and cannot be ignored. Some of the things you could do to improve your appearance are:
    i. Wardrobe improvement
    ii. Change your hair-style
    iii. Better use of cosmetics
    iv. Getting into good physical shape and looking healthy.
11. **Become Physically Healthy:** Be physically in good shape. Working out is good for your attitude. Play games; Engage in Sports activities; go for long walks; Play Badminton, Tennis, etc. Statements like "My workout does as much for my mental state as it does for my body" and "Exercise tones up my body and tunes my outlook" bear ample testimony to the deep connection between physical well-being and Attitude.
12. **Focus on the Good:** We all have some strength; we all do certain things very well; we all have at least a few happy, exciting events in our life. The more we focus on them, the better it is for our attitude. To maintain and tune up our attitude and become more

positive; we need to do three simple things: -

a. Think more about our winners - like things we do well.
b. Talk about our winners - Verbalize happy, exciting events of our life and not drone on endlessly about the negatives of our situation.
c. Reward ourselves by enjoying our winners — consistently and constantly enjoy your winners, for e.g., Playing Golf or music, etc.

13. **Don't keep your P.A to yourself:** Spread your P.A. Give your P.A. to others. Be generous with your P.A When you share your P.A. with others; you keep and maintain your P.A. Thus, you can be generous and selfish at the same time. You can do this in simple ways like sharing your excitement with others; Visiting friends; paying compliments; cracking jokes; sending cards, etc.
14. **Have a purpose, A Vision, A Mission:** A person with a purpose in Life is more likely to have a positive attitude than someone without direction. A mission, a purpose provides direction; helps to achieve focus; dissipates fears; provides perspective and destroys uncertainty. All these help a person to get a stronger grip on his attitude.

Chapter 4

SELF ESTEEM / SELF IMAGE

We all have our own Self-Image. According to Zig Ziglar, a healthy self-image is the starting point for success, prosperity and happiness. Dr. Joyce Brothers, well-known author, columnist and psychologist says: "An individual's self-concept is the core of his personality. It affects every aspect of human behaviour: the ability to learn, the capacity to grow and change, the choice of friends, mates and careers. It's no exaggeration to say that a strong positive self-image is the best possible preparation for success in Life".

We work and live within our self-image. It controls our Status, our Income, our Social Prestige, our Performance, etc. The authors Dorothy Jongeward and Muriel James in their well-known book "Born to Win" say that "man was born to win, but throughout a lifetime, as a result of our negative society, he is conditioned to lose". They also emphasize the fact that a healthy self-image is an essential prerequisite for success. Self-esteem is the deep-down feeling that you have of yourself. It is how you rate yourself from the depth of your being. We all perform according to the image we have of ourselves. It is impossible to act otherwise. We cannot consistently perform in a manner that is inconsistent with the way we see ourselves. Thus, to rise to your full potential, you have to change the "Inside Image". This is basic and of paramount importance because the mind completes whatever picture we put into it. Therefore, you must learn to see yourself the way you want to be and clearly visualize what you want to do. It is not what you are that holds you back — it's what you think you are not that holds you back. You must feel, from deep down within you that you deserve, absolutely deserve, wealth, prosperity, abundance, happiness, success, achievement, rich inter-personal relationship, etc. before these things will be yours. Motivation, goal-setting, positive thinking, etc. also will not work for a person with a poor self-image. It is important to note that we are talking about a healthy self-image and self-acceptance and not about an inflated ego.

Before we discuss the steps to build a healthy self-image, it would be worthwhile to briefly sum up the causes of a poor self-image and its manifestations.

Causes of a Poor Self-Image: - Zig Ziglar enumerates the following causes of a poor self-image:-

A. We are constantly bombarded with negativities from all sides because we generally deal with negative individuals in a negative society.

B. We are victims of "devastating put-downs" by parents, teachers, friends and others in authority, who repeatedly ridicule or question our ability, appearance and intelligence,

C. The 3rd cause of poor self-image is the tendency to confuse failure in an event or a project with failure in life

D. Another cause for a poor self-image is comparing your worst feature, to someone else's best feature

E. Another cause is an unrealistic and unfair comparison of experiences. We exaggerate the successful experiences of others and downgrade our own success.

F. Lastly, people have a poor self-image because they set standards of perfection that are unrealistic and unreachable. Thus, they set themselves up for failures.

Expressions or Manifestations of a poor Self-Image: -

It will not be wrong to say that every area of life and every occupation is adversely affected by a poor self-image. People with poor self-image are generally critical and jealous by nature. They tend to gossip a lot and tend to stoke the fires of rumours with baseless and untrue comments. They also reveal their deeply felt insecurities by resenting the praises or recognition which others may receive. A person with a poor self-image is very uncomfortable when he is alone or inactive. He has an almost compulsive need to go somewhere or do something. He cannot calmly sit alone by himself. When alone, he will keep the radio or TV on even if he is not watching or listening. People with poor self-image often over-eat and become obese, dress unattractively, do not bother about personal hygiene, often take to drugs or alcohol. Surprisingly, sometimes a poor self-image is manifested by flaunting flashy cars, money, the current fad, way-out clothes, hairdos and make-up. A salesman will exhibit his poor self-image by, amongst other things, his reluctance to close the sale. A businessman would reveal his self-image by making 'impossible' promises and a parent with a poor self-image would display reluctance to discipline a child.

Steps to Build a Healthy Self-Image: - Regardless of how poor our self-image is, we can all improve it and choose the way we want to be. To build your self-esteem, do everything and anything that makes you feel, good. A few suggestions: -

1. **Smile**: - In every language, in every culture it reflects the light in your window that tells people that there's a caring, sharing individual inside. It is an international pass¬port. A smile definitely increases your "Face" value. When you smile at someone and he smiles back, you automatically feel better.
2. **Compliment People:** - Be generous in complimenting others. When you sincerely compliment a person, it makes him feel better. This, in turn will make you feel better. Accept compliments graciously. Never

disregard a compliment. If you do that, you devalue yourself.

3. **Spread Optimism and Good Cheer:** - Be Joyous. Greet People with and respond to their greetings with joy and enthusiasm. Likewise, talk with enthusiasm and energy on the telephone. Even if you are not feeling good, pretend and act as if you are feeling good. Feelings will follow action and soon you will start feeling good.
4. **Dress and Look your best at all times:** - A well-groomed person communicates to the world that he is thorough, efficient and has high personal standards. Moreover, your outward appearance affects your image and your performance. The way you look externally has a definite effect on how you feel and see yourself on the inside. The better you look, the better you feel. A good outside appearance enhances the potential and performance of a person while a poor external appearance cripples them. Also, work to be healthy/slim and trim. Many former obese people have reported great improvement in their self-image with weight loss. In the same vein, plastic surgery can also be helpful in some circumstances.
5. **Volunteer your name first in every communication:** - Telephone or face to face and whenever you meet someone new. Announce your name always with pride, joy and enthusiasm. By paying value to your name, you are developing the habit of paying value to yourself.
6. **To build up your self-image, list out your positive qualities:** - Write them on a card and refer to it often. Be aware of your strengths. List out your personality traits which you like about yourself. Likewise, list your talents and character traits which you like about yourself. And also, ask your friends and family to list

the things they like about you. Keep those lists handy. As Zig Ziglar says "Brag on you from time to time to build a healthy self-image".

7. **Keep a record of your past Successes, Victories and Accomplishments:** - List them out. Periodically, review this list. This will serve to remind you that since you have succeeded in the past, you can succeed again. This knowledge builds confidence, which builds image, successes, and happiness. Keep adding to this list.
8. **Learn Public Speaking:** - Public speaking is a tremendous confidence booster. Acquiring the ability to stand up and speak in public is one of the best, quickest and most effective ways to improve your image and performance. Public speaking skills will also help you to meet different life situations more confidently.
9. **Always stand tall and walk erect and briskly:** - This will communicate to the world that you are confident about yourself and know where you are going.
10. **Upgrade your skills:** - Acquire professional competence. Be amongst the Best in your field
11. **Use affirmative, encouraging language when you talk to yourself and others about yourself:** - Everything you say about yourself is sub-consciously being recorded by yourself and more importantly, by your self-image.
12. **Keep a Self-Development plan ongoing at all times:** - Seek out the real winners in life as friends and role models. In particular, learn from those historical figures who had more than their share of failures, notwithstanding which they reached the pinnacle of success - men like Henry Ford, Thomas Edison, Albert Einstein, Abraham Lincoln, Walt Disney, etc.

13. **Choose your Associates wisely and carefully: -** Make a conscious effort to associate with achievers- who are optimistic and always look at the bright side of life. Avoid persons who have negative attitudes and beliefs and who only dump negative garbage into your mind. Associating with the "right" people is very important because we tend to imbibe and acquire much of the thinking, mannerisms and characteristics of the people we mingle with.
14. **Avoid Negative Influences:** Everything that goes into your mind has an effect and is permanently recorded. Therefore, avoid not only negative people but also books, movies, T.V Programs, newspapers which have negative connotations and portray mankind at its worst. It is a cinch that when you view mankind at its worst, you will feel that your own value has diminished. For the same reason, avoid pornography.
15. **Take Baby Steps:** Start small, Score small victories. Make incremental growth. Build up your self-image step by step. Don't aim for big victories in the beginning. Don't venture into difficult or unknown territory. Work in your area of strength. Work in the area where you have a high possibility of success. Once you achieve success, you can move another step and another and another. Each step, each success gives added confidence and as Zig Ziglar says, "Your self-image, which improves your performance, which improve your self- image, which improve performance which, improve....". David - McClelland, a psychologist at Harvard, names this "Accomplishment Feedback".
16. **Read Biographies and Autobiographies:** The true-life stories of people who triumphed over heavy odds and crushing circumstances and achieved tremendous success will inspire and help you to visualize yourself

performing commendably.

17. **Help Others:** Do something for someone else. It will boost your self -image significantly. According to Zig Ziglar, to be more effective two conditions must be fulfilled

    A. You must accept no compensation.

    B. The person or persons you assist should not be in a position to do anything for you in return.

18. Set your own internal standards, rather than comparing yourself with others. Keep upgrading your own standards in lifestyles, behaviour, professional accomplishment, relationships, etc.
19. Stand in front of a full-length mirror and tell yourself with enthusiasm "I LIKE MYSELF" at least 3-5 times a day.
20. Hug yourself at least 3-5 times a day saying, "I LOVE MYSELF".
21. Respond to your every small success, every small achievement with a pat on the back accompanied by an enthusiastic "Well Done" or "Shabash".
22. Every day do something that will make you happy.
23. Don't bother about what others may be thinking about you. That is none of your business. Deliberately create situations to overcome the fear of what others think.
24. Always treat yourself well. Give yourself a treat whenever possible — Buy good clothes, books, audio-cassettes, go to a good restaurant, visit the beauty parlour, etc. Remember you deserve, absolutely deserve, the best.
25. Learn to say "No" when you have to/want to and feel good about it. Don't feel guilty about it or indulge in self-reproach over it.
26. Allow yourself to "Relax" when you "Need" to

without feeling guilty about it.

27. To improve your Self-Image, practice Affirmations and Visualizations. Use your Power of Imagination. Mentally rehearse every performance before you actually perform. There is the true story of a man who practiced Golf-mentally-for several hours in prison and improved considerably. In their imagination, winners see what they want; losers see what they don't want. Winners dwell on their wins [What went right]; losers dwell on their losses [What went wrong]. Therefore, always "Picture in your mind, the world you want to see". See what you want and get what you see. Every success is created twice: First in your mind and then in the outside world.

Chapter 5

SELF-CONFIDENCE

What is self-confidence? It is not arrogance! It is not boasting or throwing your weight around. Self-confidence is the assurance, the inner feeling of being able to get the desired result in any situation. It is a feeling of trust in one's abilities, qualities and judgement. It is a feeling of assurance arising from appreciation of one's own uniqueness (not comparing yourself with others). It is a combination of self-acceptance and unconditional positive regard.

A self-confident person is an assertive person. Assertiveness is the ability to speak of personal concerns without anger or passivity. It is standing up for your rights and expressing your thoughts, feelings, beliefs and wants in a direct, honest and appropriate way, while respecting the rights of others and being responsive to their needs. In short, assertiveness means your ability to act in harmony with your self-esteem, without hurting others.

Signs of self-confidence

- A pleasant demeanour
- A cheerful outlook on life
- A wide circle of friends
- Satisfaction with one's personal life
- Relaxed, enthusiastic and energetic
- Display of inner strength polished with social skills

Why do we need self-confidence?

- Building self-confidence will determine the level of responsibility a person takes and the initiative he exercises.
- All achievements and success in the external world depend on it.
- Quality of one's relationships depend on it.
- You strike a win-win deal with others; you look after yourself and others too.
- Your trust/belief in yourself, in life, in others, helps unfold your dreams and potential.

Confidence is the ability to rise above negative feelings, failures and mistakes. Believe in yourself actively, not passively. Confidence comes from belief. What we need immediately is self-belief. What is a belief? It is a thought etched in stone. It is necessary to believe in yourself and in your capacity to perform to the best of your ability, even if others, including so-called experts, treat you with contempt. A winner is not one who never fails, but one who never quits! We give below, five real-life examples of persons who achieved tremendous success, because of self-belief, in spite of being rejected by so-called experts, by people in authority:

- A candidate for a news broadcaster's post was rejected by officials since his voice was not fit for a news broadcaster. He was also told that with his obnoxiously long name, he would never be famous. He is **Amitabh Bachchan.**
- A small boy — the fifth among seven siblings of a poor father — was selling newspapers in a small village to earn his living. He was not exceptionally smart at school but was fascinated by religion and rockets. The first rocket he built, crashed. A missile that he built crashed multiple times and he was made

a butt of ridicule. He is the person to have scripted the space odyssey of India single-handedly. He is **Dr. APJ Abdul Kalam.**

- In 1962, four nervous young musicians played their first record audition for the executives of the Decca Recording Company. The executives were not impressed. While turning down this group of musicians, one executive said, “We don’t like their sound. Groups of guitars are on the way out.” This group was called **The Beatles.**
- In 1944, Emmeline Snively, Director of the Blue Book Modeling Agency, told modeling hopeful Norma Jean Baker, “You’d better learn secretarial work or else get married.” She went on to become **Marilyn Monroe.**
- In 1954, Jimmy Denny, manager of the hotel, Grand Ole Opry, fired a singer after one performance. He told him, “You ain’t going nowhere, son. You ought to go back to driving a truck.” The singer went on to be known as **Elvis Presley.**

The moral of the above stories: Character cannot be developed in ease and quiet. Only through experience of trial and suffering can the soul be strengthened, vision cleared, ambition inspired, and success achieved. You gain strength and confidence by every experience where you really stop to look fear in the face. You must do the thing you cannot do. And remember, the finest steel gets sent through the hottest furnace. In life, remember that you pass this way only once! Let’s live life to the fullest and give it our extreme best.

Four reasons to believe in yourself

No one else will

If you don’t believe in yourself, how do you expect anyone

else to believe in you? Your self-confidence and self-esteem stem from a strong belief in who you are and what you stand for. It is important to remember that you are your number one supporter and fan.

You owe it to yourself

The best thing you can do for yourself is believing in yourself. It is a great feeling to have affirmative thoughts about yourself. Believing in yourself is a 'yes' thought that goes a long way to accelerate positive progress in your life. You are your own best friend; expect good things from and for yourself.

Life is what you make it

Believing that you can make it happen for yourself is an important step towards making a life that you like. You must believe that you can do it and that you will succeed. Life is a do-it-yourself project. A lot of decisions you make and things you do depend on you; so, arm yourself with self-belief, make the right choices and make it happen!

You have dreams and aspirations

What will happen to them if you don't believe in yourself and in your capacity to fulfil them? If you have a passion to fulfil your dreams and aspirations, do not allow them to go waste just because you don't believe in yourself.

Beliefs can be positive or negative, empowering or disempowering, expanding or limiting. It is crucial to distinguish a belief from a factual statement. For example, saying "I don't know how to operate computers" may be a statement of fact, but saying "I can never learn how to operate computers" is a belief. It is important to identify your negative beliefs and convert them into positive beliefs. Change 'can't' to 'can' and 'try' to 'will'.

How are beliefs formed?

Negative influences — criticism, ridicule, discrimination, unfair treatment, discouragement, defeats, crushed dreams, particularly when we were young, are the genesis of negative beliefs that we have formed about ourselves. We have learnt to limit ourselves, to crush our potential. We are born to win.

But we have conditioned ourselves to lose. To de-condition ourselves, we need to:

- Outgrow our self-imposed limitations
- Mind our self-talk
- Practice affirmations and visualization

The process of forming beliefs is a cycle — a virtuous cycle. You start with a belief which releases your potential. This leads to action, which gives results —positive results — which empower the belief which releases more potential and so on.

You may not succeed the first time or right at the beginning. But that is immaterial. Failure is final only when you give up. In fact, there is no such thing as failure. There are only results which are named success or failure. Success is the result that you desire, and failure is the result you don't desire.

Don't stop at the hurdles, jump over them. Be flexible. Beliefs make shells around us. Once you break that shell, you are free. You will be confident.

Persistence

One more quality which is essential is persistence. It means never, ever, giving up. Persist in doing a thing till you succeed. The life of Edison is an eloquent testimony to this quality. He failed hundreds of time, and every time, his response was "I know one more way it does not work" and "Every time I hear a 'no', it brings me closer to the 'yes' I want," and "Success is a series of 'no's' with a 'yes's' at the end of it."

In other words, we need the quality and attitude of WITTS: Whatever It Takes to Succeed. We are all born with confidence and WITTS. That is how we learn to walk, talk, read, eat, etc. We need to regain these qualities if we have lost them in the process of living.

Decision

The next thing is to decide to change. Life is a series of choices/decisions. We are constantly making decisions in life. Yet, we make no more than a few big/major decisions in a lifetime; perhaps only about 5-10. But we do make a whole lot of small, minor decisions and life changes because of these. Decisions regarding dress, hairstyle, food habits, waking/sleeping, backbiting, reading, watching TV, exercising, etc. impact our life. So, what is needed is that we consistently make empowering choices and correct small decisions. Little tweaks to your lifestyle and thought process will create major changes in your life.

Blocks to a more confident you

- Self-doubts, negative self-talk, put-downs, blaming yourself, devaluing yourself
- Lack of self-respect
- Lack of appreciation (personal or environmental)
- Unequal comparisons with others (your half-empty glass with their full glass)
- Lack of competence or skills
- Fears and anxieties
- Failures in life

Tips to a more confident you

- Exercise and eat healthy.
- Maintain positive attitude and indulge in positive self-talk. Change ‘can’t do’ to ‘can do’.
- Learn new activities and skills.
- Appreciate your uniqueness.

- Turn envy/jealously into a desire to achieve.
- Develop and nurture an attitude of gratitude.
- The principal goal in life is to be happy and confidence is a state of happiness. Practice being happy and begin with a smile.
- Enthusiastically visualize that you are a positive, confident person.
- Each time you initiate action, always remember successful experiences from the past- When you evoke these feelings, you will feel successful and act with confidence. Each time, say, "I am confident" and this, in turn, will evoke feelings of confidence instantly.
- Accept all your negative feelings as a challenge. Confidence is the ability to rise above negative feelings, failures and mistakes.
- Believe in yourself actively, not passively, confidence comes from belief.
- Create an aura of self-confidence around you by displaying good body language (posture, gestures, eye contact), presenting an attractive appearance, manners and etiquette and good communication skills (both listening and speech).

Things that will help

- Write one page daily— whatever comes to your mind —first thing in the morning. Do not worry about spelling, grammar, etc. Just write. Do this for at least a month. This will help to unburden guilt, fear and resentment which clog your self-confidence.
- Spread happy, positive words. When you say, "I feel good", you start feeling good. When you are asked or greeted with "How are you?" or "How do you feel?"

reply enthusiastically with "Awesome! "Fantastic/ wonderful/on top of the world and not just "ok", "no problem" or "getting along".

- Smile at people — smile big — open yourself to the world. The principal goal in life is to be happy: Practice being happy with a smile. Remember, confidence is a state of happiness.
- Fake confidence till you make it.
- Learn public speaking. It is a tremendous confidence booster.
- Convince yourself that you are important. If you were important, how would you talk/walk/feel? When you have pictured these things, put them into practice.
- Set goals. Choose easy goals in the beginning. Fulfil them. This will improve self-confidence and competence.
- Take interest in others, care for them, get involved with their interests. As you lose yourself in others, you will find your self-confidence restored.
- Socialize —join clubs and networking organizations. This will give you a sense of belonging and a sense of accomplishment.
- Forget your failures. Learn from them and move on.
- Always remember your successes and build on them.
- Reward yourself whenever you succeed, no matter how small the victory. This will increase your success consciousness and give fillip to your self-confidence.
- Talk to your loved ones — they boost your Morale.
- Be optimistic. Always expect the best.
- Focus on your strengths, also work on your weaknesses.
- Smile big: it gives you confidence.

- Practice speaking up —take part in discussions, ask questions, contribute to the discussion by speaking up and expressing your thoughts and opinions. It is a confidence-building vitamin. Speak up at every meeting/discussion.
- Be a front-seater, sitting upfront builds confidence.
- Practice eye contact. Lack of eye contact shows lack of confidence.
- Walk 25 % faster. Slovenly posture and sluggish walking show unpleasant attitude. You can change your attitude by changing posture and speed of movement.
- Read self-improvement and motivational books and also listen to audios and watch videos dealing with self-development and motivation.
- Practice affirmation and visualization.
- Have/develop high self-esteem.
- Believe that you deserve the best.
- Don't compare yourself with others. Instead, compare against your own past record.
- Acquire new skills. Take up a social activity such as dancing, playing tennis, etc.
- Don't compare your weakness against the strong point of others.

Chapter 6

INTER-PERSONAL SKILLS

Developing Good Human Relations [Getting along with people]

President Theodore Roosevelt said: "The most important single ingredient to the formula of success is knowing how to get along with people".

John Rock Feller stated: "I will pay more for the ability to deal with people than for any other ability under the sun".

According to Shiv Khera, "People knowledge is more important than product knowledge".

According to A.H.Smith, President of a leading railroad company in the U.S.A - "A railroad is 95% man and 5% iron". It is estimated that an average executive spends 3/4th of his working day dealing with people.

It is vital to remember that: a] The largest single cost in most business is people; b] The biggest, most valuable asset any company has is its people; c] All the plans of Top Management are carried out by or fail to be carried out by its employees.

People, in the know of things maintain that "if you learn how to deal with people — it is 85% of the way on the road to success in any organization and 99% on the way down the road to personal happiness".

Thus, if you want to be a success in life — no matter what

goals you have or profession you choose — you must learn to develop positive relations with people.

A few simple tips to Build Good Relationships [Develop Positive People Skills]

1. **Appreciate People:** You can always find something positive in others which you can appreciate. Be sincere. Be honest. Give sincere appreciation — not flattery. Appreciation makes a person feel important. The desire to feel important is one of the deepest desires of most human beings. According to William James, the renowned psychologist, "One of the deepest desires of human beings is the desire to be appreciated. The feeling of being unwanted is hurtful". Mother Teresa says, "The biggest disease today is not leprosy or tuberculosis but rather the feeling of being unwanted".
2. **Acknowledge People for what they have done:** say "Thanks" sincerely and meaningfully. Get into the habit of thanking people enthusiastically, politely and courteously. Don't take people for granted. Be grateful. Express gratitude. But don't expect or insist on gratitude from others.
3. **Ask Forgiveness:** Admit mistakes, say, "I am Sorry" whenever you are wrong. Admit it quickly.
4. **Forgive People:** When they are in the wrong, forgive them without their asking. It is in your own interest to do so, don't be egoistic. Ego leads to arrogance. Ego loves misery. A happy person has no ego. Ego is the biggest hurdle in building a positive relationship.
5. **Let Go:** Learn to let go of many things at the earliest. Don't hold on to grievances / hurts / resentments.
6. **Avoid Arguments:** Arguments cause damage. You can never win an argument. Even if you win, you lose.

Arguments cause hurt. They leave people bitter and may make them vindictive. A discussion is healthy and positive. An argument is unhealthy and negative. In an argument, people spend their thought and energy in proving “who is wrong”; in a discussion, they try to find out “what is right”; An argument generates heat, a discussion throws light on the topic; In a discussion when one talks, the other listens; in an argument both talk and neither listens; the best way to win an argument is to avoid it.

7. **Be Cheerful:** Cheerfulness flows from goodness. Spread cheer and goodwill wherever you go, and to whomsoever you meet. Carry your own sunshine with you and there will be fewer dark places in the world.
8. **Smile:** Smile big and more often. Smile increases face value. It is the most inexpensive cosmetic and is also infectious. A smiling face is always welcome. A smile costs nothing, but it creates much. It enriches those who receive it without impoverishing those who give it. And it is worth nothing to anyone until it is given away.
9. **Stay away from Gossip:** Avoid Back-biting. Remember that a person who tattles to you about others is also likely to gossip about you to others. Therefore, avoid gossip. Gossip tarnishes reputations and causes heartaches.
10. **Don’t Pre-judge people:** Have an open, unbiased mind.
11. **Develop a Sense of Humour:** A Sense of humour makes a person likeable and attractive. Laugh with people, not at people. Better still, learn to laugh at yourself. The day you first laugh at yourself is the day you start growing. Take your work seriously, don’t take yourself too seriously. In your humour, avoid

put-downs, sarcasm and hurtful remarks. Don't make fun of others. It shows poor taste.

12. **Practice Empathy:** Put yourself in the other person's shoes. See things from the other person's point of view. Do this and your relationship will improve — be it with your friends, your sibling, your colleague, your boss/sub-ordinate, your spouse, etc. Empathy not only improves relationships, it also generates understanding, loyalty, peace of mind and higher productivity.
13. **Remember People's Names:** A person's name is the sweetest word for him
14. Avoid the 3 "C's"- The 3 "Cancers" of Inter-Personal Relationship, i.e.

    a. Criticize

    b. Condemn Don't

    c. Complain

    On the other hand, always exercise "CONTROL" before speaking or writing.
15. **Learn to Listen:** Listen well. Practice listening skills. Be an Active Listener. Encourage people to talk. Listen not only to what is "Said" but also to what is "Not Said". Listen to verbal as well as non-verbal communication.

    Listen without Interruption
    Listen without Judgment
    Listen without Opinions
    Listen without Invalidation
16. **Don't try to change others:** Instead, change yourself for the better.
17. **Make the Other person feel important and do it sincerely:** Give the other person praise and respect.
18. **Let the other person save his/her face:** Call attention

to other people's mistakes indirectly.

19. **Be a Giver:** Give more and you will get more. Give for the joy of giving — not to get something in return. Give freely and fearlessly. Relationships are like Bank Accounts. The more we deposit, the greater they become.
20. **Take your Focus off yourself:** The Potential for good relationships increases when you begin focusing on others.
21. **Care a Lot about People:** "People don't care how much you know until they know how much you care". Have genuine heartfelt care for others. A person all wrapped up in himself makes a pretty small package.
22. **Know a Lot about them:** It is a sign that you care, and it creates a positive, lasting bond. It is said that Napoleon not only knew every officer in his army by name, but he also knew details about their home/family lives.
23. **Don't under-estimate the value of any Individual you deal with:** Always value those who are present. Relate to their positives, their strengths from your positives and your strengths. Meet each person with positive anticipation and expect every encounter to yield positive results. Treat everyone as important.
24. **Always be Courteous and Polite:** Courtesy means consideration for the feelings of others. Courtesy is reflected in good manners. Courtesy shows good upbringing. It is a sign of being refined, polished and cultured. Small courtesies will improve relationships and take a person far. It is also desirable to lavishly use "Courtesy" words like "Thank You", "Please", "Sorry", etc. Words have great impact. Therefore, choose your words carefully. Words can build up relationships. They can also hurt feelings and break

relationships. Therefore, choose what you say rather than say what you choose.

Use the following and similar sentences as frequently as possible.

[Judge the appropriateness for yourself]

1. Thank you very much
2. I am sorry. Please forgive me.
3. Let me help you or I would like to help you.
4. Wow! You look great / terrific [idea is to appreciate]
5. I am so proud of you.
6. I missed you so much
7. How sweet is your child / kid!
8. Go ahead. I am with you.
9. Let's go out for Lunch / Dinner [i.e. acknowledge some good work done]
10. I Love you so very much.

25. **Seek to understand first before insisting on being understood:** To be "Understood" is a deep-felt human need. Try to "Understand" the other person first before insisting that you are "Understood" first.

26. **Be Credible and Consistent:** Breaking trust damages friendships / relationships. Being inconsistent — i.e. when words and actions don't match — leads to loss of credibility. And lost credibility not only damages friendships, it also destroys business relationships. People we deal with will act more willingly and co-operate more readily if our credibility is beyond question. Ability is important — dependability is critical.

27. **Don't take Undue Advantage of People:** Besides being wrong, it simply doesn't work. Advancing yourself at the expense of others only gives the

illusion of success. In the long run it hurts you as well as others.

28. **Ask for Advice or Special Favours:** People love the opportunity to show their expertise and they enjoy the feeling that comes when they can help you from a position of power or authority.

29. **Always bring something to the Table:** The best relationships are those where both parties are giving to and receiving from each other — ideas, encouragement, books, business opportunities, material for personal growth, etc. The desire or motivation should be to help the other person with his goals. And as Ralph Waldo Emerson says, "it is one of the most beautiful compensations of life that no man can sincerely try to help another without helping himself". Goodness has a way of coming back. Zig Ziglar says, "You can get everything you want in life, if you help enough other people get what they want".

30. **Be Considerate of People's Feelings:** Man is not only a "Creature of Logic" — a rational being — but he is also a "bundle of emotions". People are emotional beings. Therefore, be considerate of their emotions. Dr. Paul Parker said, "You can handle people more successfully by enlisting their feelings than by consulting their reasons".

31. **Talk in terms of the Other Person's Interest** and not try to interest the other person in yourself. Focus your attention on the other person's interests — Pictures, Books, Trophies, Vocation, Profession, etc. and if there are common areas where your interests and his converge, then the conversation will become richer and both parties will enjoy the relationship twice as much.

32. In conclusion, let me give you what can be termed as,

"A short course in Relationship Building": -

- The Six Most Important words.......
  "I Admit I Made A Mistake"
- The Five Most Important Words.........
  "You Did A Good Job".
- The Four Most Important Words.......
  "What Is Your Opinion"? Or "What Do You Think"?
- The Three Most Important Words.......
  "If You Please" I "You Are Right".
- The Two Most Important Words.......
  "Thank You".
- The One Most Important Word......
  "WE"
- The Least Important Word....
  "I"

The essence of good human relations can be summed up in the following story:

A little boy was angry with his mother. He ran out of the house, went up the valley and shouted, "I hate you, I hate you", and back came the echo, "I hate you, I hate you". The boy got frightened because he had never heard an echo before in his life. He ran back to his mother and told her that there was a wicked boy in the valley who shouted, "I hate you, I hate you". The mother asked her son to go back and shout, "I love you, I love you". The little boy ran up the valley again and shouted, "I love you, I love you", and back came the echo "I love you, I love you". The lesson to be learnt from the story is that "our life is like an echo: We get back what we give". No wonder Benjamin Franklin said, "When we are good to others, we are best to ourselves".

Chapter 7

GOALS AND GOAL SETTING

Goals are the building blocks of success. Without goals, you leave success to chance. Well defined goals backed up by confident, enthusiastic action are the building blocks of achievement. According to Jim Dorman, without goals "Success is unattainable because success is actually the attainment of these goals".

Success means different things to different people. For some it may be accumulating wealth; to others it may be Fame or acquiring Professional Excellence; to still others it may be becoming an outstanding sportsperson or Film Star. We regard success as "the progressive realization of worthwhile, pre-determined personal goals". This definition can work for anyone no matter what his focus in life is. It also permits one to tailor success to one's personal values and vision.

The strongest force in human motivation is setting goals. They give you meaning, purpose, direction, focus. When you set goals for yourself, they work in 2 ways. You work on them and they work on you. Goals help you to concentrate on the most important activities; to use your time most productively. They help you to assess the various demands made on your time and energy and reduce or drop the superfluous, extraneous demands and the unimportant pulls and pressures.

It is a tragic fact that out of the more than 4 billion people who inhabit this planet, only a very small minority have their lives well under control and are doing what they want to do and should be doing. Jim Dorman says: "98 out of 100 persons who are dissatisfied with their world do not have a clear picture in their minds of what they would like. They have no goal for a better life."

Research workers in America asked the captains of 100 ships, where they would be six months hence and how far they would travel. Interestingly, 97% of them knew exactly where they would be in six months' time. The researchers asked the same questions to the graduates of Boston University at their convocation. Sadly, 97% of the graduates were unable to state clearly what they would be doing six months hence. Without a sense of purpose, you are likely to go nowhere in life. J.C. Penny said: "give me a Stock Clerk with a goal and I will give you a man who will make history. Give me a man without a goal, and I will give you a Stock Clerk'".

Goal-Setting helps you to lift the lid on yourself and maximize your potential. Goals also give you the power to live in the present; to keep your priorities straight and shift your emphasis from activity to output and accomplishment; to focus on the important things and not get lost in the maze of urgent activities. Without goals, you may tend to confuse Busyness with Achievement.

There is a vast difference between Activity and Accomplishment. A French Scientist named Henri Faber experimented with Recessionary Caterpillars. A caterpillar wants to follow the one in front of it blindly. Faber arranged some caterpillars in a circle in the flower pot in such a way that the lead caterpillar was right behind the last one forming the circle. He put food for the caterpillars in the centre of the flower pot. The caterpillars kept on going around in a circle in the flower pot. Finally, after about seven days of busily circling around, they dropped dead of starvation and exhaustion with enough food only a few inches away from them.

The lesson to be learnt by us is that just because we are engrossed in an activity, in doing something, it does not mean that we are progressing or achieving something. We must evaluate our activity in order to ensure accomplishment.

Shiv Khera narrates the following two stories in this connection:

a) A man was driving with his wife and the wife said, "Honey, we are going the wrong way." The husband replied, "Who cares, we are making a great time!"

   He concludes that if we confuse activity with accomplishment, we could be making great time, but we won't get anywhere.

b) A farmer had a dog that used to sit by the roadside waiting for vehicles to come around. As soon as one came, the dog would run down the road barking and trying to overtake it. One day a neighbour asked the fanner: "Do you think your dog is ever going to catch a car?" The farmer replied, "That is not what bothers me. What bothers me is what he would do if he ever caught one".

Shiv Khera observes: "Many people in life behave like that dog who is pursuing meaningless goals".

Goals bring out the best qualities in you. They display your desire to become better, to 'become more productive, to improve and to achieve. It shows your vision to make your future better than your present or your past.

There are six important/major areas in a person's life viz:

a. Family and Home
b. Profession and Finances
c. Mental wellness and Education
d. Societal and Cultural
e. Physical wellbeing and Health
f. Ethical and spiritual

It is important to balance and prioritize your goals. [The relative importance of each area may differ from person to person and, from time to time, for the same person]. When you set goals in all these major areas, you ensure that you do not give undue or exaggerated importance to any one area of your life. This will make your life more "balanced" as your "Wheel of Life" will be more rounded and will "Roll" more smoothly.

Your goals should be "SMART" Goals: -

S - Specific and not vague and general
M - Measurable
A - Attainable
R - Realistic
T - Time-bound

a) Specific: For e.g., saying "I want to be rich" is very vague and general. The specific goal would be "I am going to have Rs. 1 Crore in my bank account by ...."

b) Measurable: Your goal must be measurable. Any goal that cannot be measured is no goal at all. For e.g.,

i. I will become a wonderful boss
ii. I want to become a fantastic speaker
iii. I want to become an ideal husband/wife/child
iv. I want to become an excellent human being

These statements are not measurable because "Wonderful Boss", etc. cannot be measured. Hence, there is scope for non-performance. It is imperative to clearly specify what we mean by "Good Boss". For e.g., "I will increase the Turnover of the company from .... To ...."

In this connection, it is relevant to draw attention to Florence Chadwick who was a Champion Swimmer. She had conquered the English Channel. On July 4, 1952, she attempted to swim the Catalina Channel. It was chillingly cold, and a dense fog enveloped the surroundings. She struggled to reach the shore. It was so dense that she was unable to see the shore. She gave up. She quit not because she was a quitter but because she could not see her goal. Later on, she found out that she was only a short distance away from the coast when she quit. She blurted Out "Look I am not excusing myself. But if I could have seen land, I might have made it". Florence Chandwick was a great swimmer, but she still needed a goal she could see to motivate her. Thus, goals should be measurable. Interestingly, Florence Chandwick went back and swam the Catalina Channel in spite of bad weather.

c) Attainable: Your goals must be practical. They must be challenging but attainable. You must believe, feel that you can reach them if you stretch yourself. Otherwise, you will not make the effort. You must take into consideration your own past. For e.g. If a company's Turnover is 10 million this year, it is not probable that it can become 100 million next year. Or, 39 % student last year cannot become 93% this year.

d) Realistic: This means that there must not be anything in the outside world which militates against your goal and renders it impossible of achievement. For e.g., a 40-year old man cannot make a goal of becoming an I.A.S. Officer where the laws and rules of the country stipulate 30 years as the maximum age limit for entry into the I.A.S. Cadre. The person may have the ability to get an entry in the I.A.S. Cadre, but the law/rules prohibit the same.

e) Time-bound: You must fix a time-limit for the achievement of your goal. Without Time-limit it will only be a dream, not a goal. An example of a goal with Time-limit: John F. Kennedy's Goal: "We will put a man on the moon by the end of the year." This goal is both specific and time-bound. Another example: "I will bring my weight down to 66 Kgs by 30th Oct 2009". On the other hand, saying "I want to reach a Turnover of 20 million" has no meaning unless and until you specify a Time-Frame.

Additionally, your goals must be flexible. As you change, so will your Goals. Be flexible. Goals are your slave. You are not the slave of your goals. For e.g., If you are a student and have secured 35% last year in the finals and have fixed your goal for 65% this year for the Finals. However, in the meantime you have secured 66% in the Terminal Exams this year, you can now make an upward revision and fix your goal at, say, obtaining 80%. Another example, - Supposing a company's Turnover was 10 million last year, you have set a goal of 20 million this year. Now, in the first six months of this financial year, you have attained a turnover of only 3 million, due to economic meltdown and recession. In such a case, you may have to revise your goal, to say, 8 to 10 million under the changed circumstances. Thus, flexibility can be upward or downward. Therefore, it is advisable to review your goals once in six months or three months.

Further, your goals must be personal. They must be your own goals and not somebody else's goals. They should mean a lot to you. Only then will they motivate you.

Your goals must always be stated in positive terms, i.e. "What you want" and not "what you don't want to happen in your life". For e.g., "I want to be healthy" can be a goal but "I don't want to be sick" cannot be a goal.

WRITTEN GOALS: - It is most important to write down your goals. The importance of written goals cannot be over-emphasized. Some hard statistics will emphatically drive home the importance of reducing your goals in writing. According to U.S.A. Govt. statistics, only 3 % of Americans are wealthy to the point of being able to have everything they want and not having to work unless they want to; 10 % of Americans are financially independent; 60% are getting by from pay-cheque to pay-cheque and 27 % get by with some form of govt. or other assistance — they need support.

The group that needs support is made up of people who typically have no goals or just, survival goals. The vast majority — the 60 % group has goals, but of a general, vaguely defined nature. The upper groups — the 10 % who are financially independent and the 3% who are wealthy are made up of people with clearly defined goals. The difference between the two groups is that the wealthy 3 % group is made up of people who put their goals in writing while the 10 % who are financially independent did not.

It is important to write down your goals because written goals increase your commitment; they help you measure your progress; they serve as a constant reminder; they keep you on track; they force you to clarify and crystallize your thinking which in turn helps you to develop definite plans of action. And as Paul Myer says: "Definite Plans Produce Definite Results'. Indefinite Plans produce little or no results".

Lastly, most of our goals are not "Out of reach", they are "Out of sight". Hence it is necessary to write our goals in as clear terms as possible and look at them/read them every day.

The main purpose of goal-setting is to help you to go from where you are to where you want to go. To go from, say, A to B, you need a map. The first thing is to know "Where am I now?" and "Where do I want to go?" And from Time to Time, you need to ask:

a) Am I on track?
b) Am I heading towards B at the right speed?
c) Is B still my goal?

Your goals can be:

i. Short-Term — up to one year
ii. Mid-Term — up to 3 years
iii. Long-Term — up to 5 years

In sum, the importance and purpose of Goal-setting are to guide you, motivate you in your quest for a better life, in your journey from "Wish to fulfilment".

A Goal-Setting Exercise

Whenever you decide to set goals, follow the simple steps noted below:

1. Write down the goals you would like to achieve in as

clear terms as possible and also set a time-limit for achieving it. [1 year, 3 years, 5 years — whatever you consider adequate]

2. Write down what action you need to take immediately to start the process of achieving your goals [in the next 24 hours, within 7 days, etc.]
3. List out the people who you think can help you achieve your goal,
4. Determine the additional knowledge, skills, and ability you will need to achieve your goal and how you will acquire them.
5. Determine the obstacles and difficulties you will have to overcome in the achievement of your goal and organize them in order of size and importance.
6. Write a paragraph on: "why you are absolutely committed to achieve your goal"? This is very important. List out as many reasons as possible why it is most important that you reach your goal. The more reasons you have, the stronger will be your motivation.
7. Make a detailed Plan — broken down by activity, and place those in appropriate time-frames. In other words, break your goal into smaller goals because goals are more easily achieved if they are broken into small ones. As Gean Gordon writes:

   "Life is hard by the Yard,
   But by the inch, it's a Cinch."
8. Take action immediately. Do something every day to move towards your goal.

Developing Priorities

When you have many goals to achieve, i.e. when you have

many important things to do, how do you decide which things are important? Follow the following Plan:

a) To determine your priorities, examine your goals. Next to each of your written goal statements, note the importance of each goal by giving it an “A”, “B” or “C”.

b) An “A” means the goal is very important to you. “B” means the goal is moderately important to you. And “C” means the goal is not really that important.

c) Read over each of your “A” goals and rank them according to their relative importance. Label the most important goal “1”, the second “2” and so on. When this task is finished, you will have a priority system for your goals.

The Last Words

It is amply evident from the foregoing that goals are very important. Therefore, begin setting goals today. Don’t underestimate the power of goals. Set the course for the future. As Robert F. Mager said: “If you are not sure where you are going, you are liable to end up some place else.” Do everything in your power to fulfil your vision. Don’t end up someplace else.

Chapter 8

TIME MANAGEMENT

Time is our most precious resource. Nothing can be more fulfilling and rewarding at the end of our lives than a sense that we have spent more of it wisely than we have wasted it.

According to Paul J Myer, "Most time is wasted, not in hours, but in minutes. A bucket with a small hole in the bottom gets just as empty as a bucket that is deliberately emptied."

Henry Ford remarked that "it has been my observation that most people get ahead during the time that others waste".

We give below a few quotes to underline the importance of Time Management:

"If you ask me what I would like to buy
— It Is Time."

- Malcolm Forbes

"The most important principle of corporate
management is Time Management."

- Thomas Waston — IBM

"Ask me for anything but Time."

- Napoleon Bonaparte

"Keep your word.
Keep you Time."

- J.R.D.Tata

"I wish my day was of 48 Hours."
- Amitabh Bachchan

Imagine the following situation: -Your Bank credits your account each morning with Rupees 86,400/-. You are free to use as much or as little of the money as you choose to. You could use it for any purpose. The only condition is that whatever amount you failed to use cannot be carried over to the next day nor could it be saved. And whether you spend none or the previous day's entire amount, the following day the Bank will give you another Rupees 86,400/-.

What would you do in such a situation? Most people would very quickly figure out a way to spend that money each day. But the smart person would quickly figure out a way to wisely invest that money on a daily basis so that he would get the greatest return in the long run.

Such a situation actually exists. You, like everybody else, receive 86,400 seconds each day, which you can spend any way you like. And if you fail to use those seconds, they are gone forever. Successful people realize the value of time. When Thomas Edison, the great inventor, was asked what the most important item in the world was, his answer was "TIME". Benjamin Franklin, the great statesman, author and inventor said "Dost thou love life? Then do not squander time, for that is the stuff life is made of". In reality,

Time Management is actually Life Management.

Characteristics of Time:

(i) **Equality:** It is given in equal measure to all. All of us receive 24 Hours each day —not a second more, not a second less. The only difference between two individuals is not how much time they have but how that time is used.

(ii) **Quality:** Time is like water, it is colourless. It has no quality of its own. You give it quality. The 24 hours that are given to you per day are like 24 empty boxes. You are free to fill it with whatever you want.

(iii) **Irreversible:** Time is irreversible. Once gone, it is gone forever. You cannot call it back.

(iv) **Not Portable:** You cannot carry it with you to use it somewhere else.

(v) **Cannot be Stored:** You cannot store it for future use.

(vi) **Cannot be Bought:** As the Chinese proverb says, "An inch of gold cannot buy an inch of time".

(vii) **Cannot be borrowed:** You cannot borrow time from somebody else like you can borrow money from him.

(viii) **Illusionary [Relativity]:** When you are engaged in activities that you enjoy doing or love to do, time appears to pass much faster that when you are doing work, you don't like or work which bores you

BENEFITS OF TIME MANAGEMENT:

Some of the benefits of Time Management are:

a. Higher Productivity and Satisfaction, both in your professional as well as Personal life.

b. Frees more time for important things: Effective Time Management creates more time for the really important things like planning, development of sub-ordinates, self-renewal and, improvement in the quality of work and Life.

c. A feeling of self-mastery: As you take actions, through effective Time Management, which move you towards the fulfilment of important goals, a feeling of self-mastery grows on you.

d. Creativity: Time Management makes the mind more focused and this leads to more creative ways of working.

e. Improved Delegation which helps to free time besides being a powerful developer and motivator of your subordinates.

f. More Energy is conserved as things get better organized.

g. Lower Stress, Higher Poise and Greater Well-Being are the additional important benefits of good time management.

SETTING PRIORITIES

The essence of Time Management lies in the ability to see, organize and execute around priorities. As Benjamin Franklin said: "If you want to enjoy one of the greatest luxuries in life, the luxury of having enough time; time to rest, time to think things through, time to get things done and know you have done them to the best of your ability, remember there is only one way. Take enough time to think and plan things in the order of their importance: Your life will take on a new zest, you will add years to your life and more life to your years. Let all your things have their places. Let each part of your work have its time." The ability to know and list priorities are the most critical time management skill any person can acquire. Pascal said, "The last thing one knows is what to put first". This is true of most people because they don't know how to rank tasks in order of priority. They believe activity means accomplishment, but nothing is further from the truth.

Maintenance and Progress Tasks:

A maintenance task is one, which once completed, will leave you in the same position as you were before. A progress task is one, which you believe will help you reach a position, which is fundamentally better than the one you are in now.

In order to make the most of your time, you must get the balance right between maintenance tasks and progress tasks. If you get bogged down with the maintenance tasks, you won't find time for the progress tasks. If you know what your priorities are this will help you to get the balance right.

Urgent & Important Tasks:

The way we use our time can also be gauged by the difference between urgent and important tasks. Maintenance tasks often seem urgent and thus it becomes easy to justify doing them. Progress tasks are seldom urgent, although they are normally very important. If tasks don't appear to be urgent one is tempted to put them off.

One important aspect of effective time management is to ensure that our sense of urgency does not cloud our understanding of what is important.

Prioritization is important at each stage of Time Management. To achieve proper prioritization, one needs to ask the following questions:

Which activities move me closer to my most important results?
Which are the high payoff activities in my life?
What can I do to be more useful to my organization?
Which activities give me the most personal satisfaction?

An effective way to prioritize our activities is to use the Time Management Matrix having two factors, i.e. Urgency and Importance.

TIME MANAGEMENT MATRIX

	URGENT	NOT URGENT
IMPORTANT	**I] ACTIVITIES** a] Crises b] Pressing Problems c] Deadline Driven Projects	**II] ACTIVITIES** a] Prevention b] PC [Production Capacity) c] Relationship Building d] Recognizing New opportunities e] Planning, Recreation
NOT IMPORTANT	**III] ACTIVITIES** a) Interruptions, Calls b] Some mail, reports c] Some meetings d] Pressing matters e] Popular Activities	**IV] ACTIVITIES** a] Trivia b] Pleasant Activities cl Time-Wasters d] Some Phone Calls e] Gossip

Quadrant I: The activities in this quadrant are both important and urgent. This is the quadrant where we manage, deliver, implement and produce, where we bring our experience and judgment to bear in responding to many needs and challenges. Due to our tendency to procrastinate, to put off doing things, many important activities become urgent. Spending too much time in Quadrant I will result in Fire-Fighting, Crisis Management, Stress and Burn-out.

Quadrant II: Consists of activities that are "important, but not urgent". This is the Quadrant of Quality. When we are in this quadrant, we do our long-range planning, we anticipate and prevent problems, and we empower others, broaden our minds and upgrade our skills through reading & continuous professional development. We also build good relationships through honest, active listening, understanding and empathy. We should increase the time that we spend in this Quadrant. Time spent here will result in Vision, Perspective, Balance, Discipline, Control, and Cultivating Hobbies.

Quadrant III: The activities in this quadrant are "Urgent, but not important". Because the activities are urgent and have to be dealt with immediately, they create the illusion of importance. In this sense, this can be regarded as the Quadrant of Deception. Interruptions by way of phone calls, drop-in visitors, and unscheduled meetings fall into this category. Effective Time-Management demands that we reduce the size of this Quadrant. Time spent here will result in short-term focus: the feeling of being out of control and victimized; shallow or broken relationships; Crisis Management.

Quadrant IV: The activities in this quadrant are neither urgent nor important. This is the Quadrant of Waste. It leads to Total Irresponsibility. Ideally, we should not be in this quadrant at all.

To improve your Time-Management skills, find out where you spend most of your time. Are you sacrificing the important for the urgent and the pleasurable? Are you confusing business and activity with accomplishment? Obviously, we should drastically reduce, if not totally eliminate Quadrant 4 activities and increase the size of quadrant 2. Likewise, we should not allow the noise of urgency to create the illusion of importance. Thus, the size of Quadrant III also needs to be reduced. Similarly, when we consider Quadrant I, we should ensure that we do not fall into the trap of thinking that just because something is urgent, it's important. One criterion to adopt is to ask yourself if the urgent activity contributes to an important objective.

Pareto Principle: Keep Pareto Principle in mind [called the 80/20 rule or the concept of the "vital few and trivia / many"] The principle states that '20% of your time spent on vital activities give 80% of your productive output, while 80% spent on trivial or routine activities give 20% results". This principle applies in all areas of our lives. For effective Time Management, we need to identify our high payoff activities and then allocate more time to them [20%] by reducing time spent on trivia / routine activities [80%]

Delegation: Delegation is one of the greatest time savers. Delegation has a strategic importance in the area of time management. Delegation means entrusting to another person a job together with the authority to do it. Thus, the delegate acts as your agent. Responsibility can be shared. But the delegator remains ultimately accountable for what happens or does not happen. Delegation begins with a deep sense of the value and limits of your own time. From that stems a strong desire to focus on priorities — the work that only you can do — and to delegate the rest. Through delegation you can leverage your time by passing responsibility for completion of work to other people.

Delegation frees time for more important tasks, allows you to plan more effectively, and helps relieve the pressure of too many jobs, too many deadlines and too little time. Moreover, it is one of the most effective ways of developing your staff. A good manager must know that delegation is a master key for better time management. Additionally, it is a great motivator, enriches jobs, improves performance and raises morale.

Time Log: Peter Drucker said: "If I were asked what one thing an executive could do that would really, and quickly, make him more effective, make him achieve more and make him enjoy what he's doing, I'd say: "Make sure you know where your time goes. Don't depend on memory, it's treacherous".

This means you must keep a record of how you are spending your time - i.e. you should maintain a Time-Log. After keeping a log for a few days, you may begin to notice opportunities for improvement. For e.g., you may discover that you are spending much more time than you thought possible on reading newspapers and trade journals or compiling routine reports. You can then reduce the time spent on reading newspapers / trade journals and the work of compiling routine reports may be delegated. The time saved can be utilized for high payoff activities.

Learn to say "NO": The word "NO" is one of the most important words to save time. Be Assertive. Learn to say "NO" to distractions, to extraneous demands, to superficial and superfluous activities. Otherwise, you will lose sight of your priorities and objectives and you will become a mere slave to the priorities of others.

Prime Time: The quality of time matters more than the quantity of time: We all have our Best or Prime Time. Your prime time essentially is the time when you do your best work. Be aware [or find out] what is your best or naturally high-quality time, so that you can employ it for high-quality work. Make the best use of your best time. You can accomplish more with less effort if you program important items at this high-performance time.

Manage Your Health: To effectively manage Time and increase productivity, it is essential to be healthy and energetic. Conserve your energy and build your health by following sensible guidelines over sleep, diet and holidays. The golden rule is, balance and moderation. Also, exercise to live more fully. You will not gain the most from your time unless you are feeling physically and mentally fit.

Managing Stress: Stress can impair your productivity and adversely affect your efforts at time management. Learn to recognize the symptoms of stress and to diagnose the underlying factors. Apply a seven-step strategy for coping with stress if it invades your life: take action; express your feelings; review priorities; accept what cannot be changed; put your experience to good use; check your time management skills; and count your blessings not your afflictions.

Committed Time: Committed time is time given over to specific purposes. The things we have to do and the places we have to be in, take up much of our time, for e.g. dressing up, shaving, waiting at the Dentist's office, travelling or commuting to and from the office, etc. Learn to use or redeem committed time by using these periods for simultaneously reading, listening to tapes, working on your lap-top, rehearsing discussions, presentations, etc.

Major Time-Wasters/Robbers

We all waste a lot of time-our most precious resource: Therefore, the first step in effective time management would be to drastically reduce the time we waste. If we take care of the minutes, the hours will take care of themselves. If you learn to control the time wasters, you increase the amount of time available to you each day: A few of the top Wasters are:

a) **Being Unorganized:** If we are unorganized, we waste a lot of time looking for things. A poll of 200 large company executives revealed that executives waste nearly six weeks a year looking for misplaced items. As Jim Dornan points out: `That means they are losing over 10% of their time each year. If you are one such person, the solution is to get organized. Either hire an efficient person to keep you organized or devise systems to keep yourself from wasting time searching for things you need. According to Jim Dornan, "One of the best rules of thumb is to throw away anything you don't need, and file everything you don't throw away.

b) **Interruptions:** Interruptions are great time wasters. In fact, according to Dr. Larry Baker, President of Time Management Centre Inc., interruptions are the greatest time wasters of executives. They are very time consuming because not only is the time of actual interruption stolen from you, but every interruption also results in extra time lost for refocusing and regrouping. We may suggest a few simple ways to reduce interruptions: -

   i) Learn to work early in the morning or late at night. There will be fewer distractions and interruptions when you do so.

   ii) Work in blocks of time. When you work in blocks of time you build up momentum and you are able to accomplish more work in a shorter period of time.

   iii) Employ an efficient Secretary or Assistant. Put someone between you and the people who regularly interrupt you.

   iv) Build or redesign your office to avoid distractions. For example, don't set up your office so that people passing by can see you through a door or window and begin talking to you without invitation.

   v) Use your telephone more effectively. Remember that the telephone is there for your convenience and not vice-versa. Use the telephone as a helpful instrument, don't become a slave to your telephone. Try to set aside a particular time during the day to answer calls. Don't be afraid to put the telephone off the hook if the situation demands. You can also arrange for your calls to be screened by junior colleagues.

vi) Negative Body Language. Use negative body language to discourage interruptions and save time. For e.g. do not sit down if you are followed into your office; do not offer tea; walk out of your cabin under the pretext of some work. Some other effective non-verbal communication would be, say, glancing at your watch; pick up your phone to indicate the end of a conversation; continue to work; hold a pen; respond only by nodding your head or change the subject, etc.

c) **Tendency to go it alone:** Other people are our single greatest resource which can help us to increase our productivity. Nonetheless, many persons do not make optimum use of this asset and try to carry the entire load they have by themselves. The answer to this is delegation and empowerment. When you delegate to others, and empower them to succeed, everyone wins.

d) **Procrastination:** Procrastination is a major time-robber [stealer]. Benjamin Franklin said: "One today is worth two tomorrows". Procrastination can be defined as putting off the doing of something that should be done intentionally and habitually. If you are a procrastinator, you are probably wasting much of your precious time. In the time that it takes most procrastinators to think about a task that must be done, worry about it, find an excuse to put it off, and then work through the guilt of not having done it, they could have already performed the task and moved on to the next activity. To overcome procrastination, adopt the "T.N.T." principle, i.e. "Today not Tomorrow". Often, the best time to take any action is "Now". Other simple tips for winning over procrastination are: Positive self-statements, avoiding perfectionism; partializing or breaking down tasks; getting organized; taking a stand; rewarding yourself; developing a routine;

using visible reminders; raising energy levels and disciplining yourself.

e) **Acting too soon:** The opposite of the tendency to put off things is the tendency to act too soon. Out of a desire to solve a problem, a person may act too soon without gathering enough facts and information and without truly understanding a problem. This can lead to major problems because a hasty decision may have to be reversed in the light of new information. "Decide in haste, repent at leisure". To overcome this tendency, one has to discipline himself. Instead of forcing yourself to act by a given time, you will need to prevent yourself from acting before a given time.

f) **Negative Emotions and Attitudes:** If you harbour negative emotions like jealousy, anger, strife, defensiveness, etc., you waste time that could be used productively, and it becomes difficult, nay, impossible to do so. If necessary, sort out your emotional issues with the help of a mental health professional. If you are a victim of negative attitude, do whatever you can to cultivate a positive attitude — i.e., reading inspirational, positive books, listening to motivational tapes, attending confidence-building seminars, etc.

g) **Regretting and Daydreaming:** These preoccupations are big time wasters. Many people waste a lot of time and energy regretting and thinking about mistakes or missed opportunities. Alternately, they daydream about the future. Every minute wasted in preoccupation is a minute lost to productivity. One should learn from past mistakes and move on quickly. Likewise, instead of daydreaming one should work towards the fulfilment of one's dream and goals. People who indulge in regrets and daydreams would do well to remember the wise words of Dag Hammarskjold: "Do not look back and do not dream about the future.

It will neither give you back the past nor satisfy your daydreams. Your duty, your reward, your destiny, are here and now".

h) **Laziness:** Many people have the problem of not being able to galvanize themselves to act, to move themselves forward in a positive direction every day. For some, it may be a motivation problem. For some, it may be a discipline problem. For others, the cause may be a laid-back temperament. Still others may have the problem of keeping track of what needs to be done and when.

You can overcome the problem of laziness by using structure. One simple method would be to use a planner which will help you to keep track, in an organized fashion, of what you have to do and when you need to do it. People who operate from home may find too many distractions — TV, radio, Phone and door bell ringing; interruptions from family members and neighbours, etc. In such cases, the only disciplinary 'step you may need is a change of setting, getting away — i.e. working away from home which will make it easier to focus. Due to laziness, some people delay starting work until it becomes too late in the day to get started. Thus, they write off the whole day without accomplishing anything. The only solution to this problem is to discipline yourself to start early. Make it a practice to start early — to eat the ugly frog first thing in the morning. Always remember that Time-Management is Self-Management.

i) **Unexpected Delays:** Unexpected delays are one of the most frustrating — and time wasting — situations that one encounters. Delays at the airport or railway terminals, delays waiting for meetings to start or being kept waiting by your doctor/lawyer/accountant, etc. The best way to confront such situations is to convert them into time opportunities. Don't ever get caught empty handed. Always carry a book with you. Carry some work with you in your briefcase. Carry a tape-recorder so that you can dictate letters or record ideas; listen to motivational/informative tapes; return phone-- calls. There are a number of ways in which you can use your waiting time productively and enjoyably. Learn to make the best use of unexpected delays. Henry Ford wisely observed that "most people get ahead during the time that others waste".

j) **Failure to know and list priorities:** Lastly and most importantly, time is not used effectively because people don't take the effort to know their priorities and list them. It is very important to determine your priorities, maintain them and act on them. Find out what are your most important activities; what gives you the highest return? What gives you the greatest reward? People naturally resist doing their work in the order of its importance. Most would rather do what is pleasant or convenient. Yet there is no single idea that better manages a person's time than doing tasks by order of importance. It is said that when Bethlehem Steel Company was not doing too well, an efficiency expert named Ivy Lee advised Charles Schwab, the president of Bethlehem Steel Company to "Write down on a piece of paper the six most important things you have to do tomorrow and number them in the order of importance". He further advised that "first thing tomorrow morning, take out the piece of paper and look at item number one. Don't look at the others; just look at number one and start working on it and stay with it until it's completed. Then take item number two the same way, then number three and so on until you have to quit for the day...and do this every working day". Charles Schwab put this idea into practice and after a few weeks sent Ivy Lee a generous cheque with a letter saying that the lesson Ivy Lee taught him was the most valuable and profitable lesson that he had ever learned in his life: It was later said that in five years this was the plan that was largely responsible for turning what was then a little-known steel company into the biggest independent steel producer in the world. And it also helped Charles Schwab make a hundred million dollars.

Some more Time-Wasters:

1. Excessive Sleeping
2. Excessive TV Watching
3. Excessive Newspaper reading
4. Excessive Movie watching
5. Excessive Chit-chatting / Gossiping
6. Excessive Socializing / Drinking
7. Indecisiveness — not taking prompt decisions — Spending too much time even on trivial matters
8. Excessive, long-winded telephone conversations. Same with face-to-face communication.
9. Poor reading speed and trying to read everything that comes on your table.
10. Writing unnecessarily lengthy notes and letters.
11. Unduly long meetings.

Few more Time-Saving Tips:

1. Deal with paper only once

   3-D Policy to reduce paper work.

   a) Do it [NOW]

   b) Delegate it

   c) Destroy it

2. Plan your work & work your Plan — failing to plan is planning to fail.
3. Prepare a To-Do List and write it down

   Schedule it

   Prioritize it

   A to-do list will help you feel organized and in control.
4. Have a place for everything and have everything in its place.
5. Combine activities to save time.
6. Work in blocks of Time
7. Always ask yourself: "Is this the best use of my time right now?"
8. Take regular refreshment breaks — food is vital for concentration.
9. Preserve energy for leisure and home life; enjoy life.
10. Take small breaks for cat-naps, for quiet time; close your eyes meditate and relax.
11. Shopping
    a) Shop with a list
    b) Shop only when your stock is over
    c) Check by phone first.
12. Keep in mind that Time-Management is doing things more effectively not just more quickly.
13. Develop reading skills. Learn speed reading.
14. In speaking, be brief and to the point; be clear:
15. In writing, be brief and concise without sacrificing clarity and completeness.
16. Meetings are an inescapable part of corporate or social enterprises. Run them in a time-effective way. Call meetings only when absolutely necessary; attend only those meeting which you must — avoid optional

meetings; control loose talk in meetings; be specific in your talk; start on time and end on time; have a specific agenda; encourage discussions but summarize it at regular intervals, etc. Whenever possible, hold meetings in a colleague's office so that you can leave when you need to.

One morning, Andrew Carnegie, the Steel Magnet interviewed 2 boys for a position. He placed a package in front of each of them and told them to unwrap the package and put the contents on the table.

One boy untied the string and kept it neatly in the drawer and kept the contents on the table. The other reached for the pair of scissors lying on the table, stripped the string, tossed it into the waste basket and quickly placed the contents on the table. Thereafter Carnegie asked them to wait outside. "Shall I hire the boy who saved the string?" asked his secretary. "No, I want to hire the other boy. The days of saving strings are over. We are time savers now" replied Carnegie.

Conclusion

We can conclude this exposition on Time-Management by saying that time after time, the dividing line between success and failure for a person comes in how well he manages his time. It's very tempting to think that a few minutes here or an hour there won't make much of a difference. But they do make a difference. According to C Neil Strait, "The management of time should be the No.1 priority for us. Without some organization of our day, it will waste away without purpose and drain away without accomplishment".

The greatest possession you have is the 24 hours directly in front of you. Have you developed a strategy that will enable you to use it to your fullest?

Time Management Check List YES /NO

1	*Do I know precisely what hours of the day I am more productive?*	***Y/N***
2	*Do I do my important tasks during these hours?*	***Y/N***
3	*Do I set priorities according to their importance rather than urgency?*	***Y/N***
4	*Am I clear about my goals? Have I ever thought about my goals?*	***Y/N***
5	*Am I aware about what I am required to do for the next six months?*	***Y/N***
6	*Do I have any urgent matters to handle during the next week?*	***Y/N***
7	*Have you made any plans in that direction?*	***Y/N***
8	*Do I evaluate my performance at work and at home?*	***Y/N***
9	*Have I done anything to regularly dispose useless magazines/documents on my desk at the office or in the cupboards at home?*	***Y/N***
10	*Have I gone through my files to remove outdated material?*	***Y/N***
11	*Have I been able to change my style of functioning in key areas of which I know that it evidences my inefficiency?*	***Y/N***
12	*Do I allocate sufficient time to plan for my day to day work?*	***Y/N***
13	*Do I delegate the work wherever I can?*	***Y/N***

Prepare your own list.
Check the list and update the same.
Be your own time manager.
Enjoy a sigh of relief and live a satisfied life.
Remember others can advise you, guide you but ultimately it is your own life. You make it or break it.

Chapter 9

ASSERTIVENESS

When Life is flowing smoothly, and people are collaborative, co-operative, friendly and considerate — then there are no problems, no difficulties. But in real life we are often confronted by people who make unreasonable demands, by people who try to manipulate us; by people who try to score over us or take unfair and undue advantage; situations in which there are conflicts and clashes of interests. In all such situations our responses, our behaviour becomes very important.

There are 3 main behavioural responses or reactions:

a) Passive or submissive Behaviour

b) Aggressive Behaviour

c) Assertive Behaviour

Passive or Submissive Behaviour is when we fail to stand up for our rights or do so in such a way that others can easily disregard us. We are submissive when we fail to express our views or feelings altogether or when we express our thoughts, beliefs and feelings in a weak and apologetic manner. A Passive person is a slave to his Fears.

Here's an example: suppose a couple of years ago, a Friend borrowed Rs. 5,000/- from you. At that time, he had lost his job. His wife was sick and hospitalized. Now he has a good job in a reputed business firm. His wife has also recouped her health and is gainfully employed in a bank. Both of them are earning good salaries. He has not yet returned your money. You need your money for an important project at home.

Passive behaviour would be that whenever you meet your friend, you talk indirectly about the things you want to buy but do not tell him directly that you need your money back to help you buy what you need.

Aggressive Behaviour is when we stand up for our own rights in such a way that we violate the rights of others; when we express our thoughts, feelings and beliefs in unsuitable and inappropriate ways, even though we may honestly believe those views to be right. An Aggressive person is a slave to his Anger. In other words, when we are Aggressive, we enhance ourselves at the expense of others and put another person down while when we are submissive or Passive we tend to put ourselves down whilst attempting to accommodate the needs and views of others.

Reverting to the above example, your behaviour would be Aggressive if at a function, you saw your friend Sunil wearing new clothes, you go up to him, hold him by the Collar, threateningly demand your money and in an insulting tone, you ask him how he dares to buy new clothes when he has to repay you your Rs. 5000/-.

On the other hand, Assertive Behaviour is when we stand up for our own rights in a way that does not violate another person's rights. It leads to an honest, open and direct expression of our point of view which, at the same time, shows that we understand the other person's position.

To continue with our example, your behaviour would be Assertive if you tell Sunil "Please Pay the money you owe me", and if he expresses his difficulties, you discuss an appropriate repayment programme including repayment in suitable instalments.

Assertiveness means speaking of personal concerns without Anger or Passivity. Assertiveness is standing up for your personal rights and expressing your thoughts, feelings, beliefs and wants in direct, honest and appropriate ways, respecting the rights of others and being responsive to their needs.

Assertiveness means your ability to act in harmony with your Self-Esteem without hurting others. Assertiveness is a willingness to express your genuine positive and negative emotions without being antagonistic to others. It is the ability to express your likes/dislikes. It means being "Authentic"; being "Honest with yourself"; being "True to Yourself"; getting in "Touch with your own Feelings".

Recognizing Assertive, Submissive & Aggressive Behaviour.

People behaving submissively are likely to: -

1. Make long, rambling statements [often justifying themselves].
2. Avoid making "I" statements or qualifying them e.g., "It's only my opinion but
3. Use other qualifying phrases or words

   e.g., Maybe.......

   Would you mind very much?

   I wonder if

   Sorry to bother you but
4. Use "Filler" words

   e.g., Uh!... Ah!... You know.... sort of..., etc.
5. Put themselves down,

   e.g., I Can't

   I am hopeless at this

   I keep trying but...
6. Use Phrases that make it easier for others to ignore their needs and wants

e.g., it's not important really,
It doesn't matter
I only meant
Never mind.

People behaving aggressively are likely to

1. Make excessive use of "I" statements
2. State their opinions as facts
   e.g., "That's Rubbish"
   "That approach won't work".
3. Use Threats: "You better do it"
   "I wouldn't take the risk
4. Put others down:
   a. You must be joking
   b. You cannot be serious
   c. That's only your opinion.
5. Make a lot of use of the words ought, must, should, have to….
6. Be Keen to attach blame to others
   e.g., it was your fault
   Well, I blame you
   You said

People behaving assertively are likely to

a. Make statements that are brief and to the point.
b. Use well considered "I" Statements.
   e.g., I think
   I Believe
   I hope

I want

I like

c. Distinguish clearly between fact and opinion

e.g., In my experience

As I see it

My opinion is

d. Avoid words like, "You should" "You Ought"

e. Use open-ended question to find out the thoughts, opinions, wants of others.

e.g., How does this affect you?

What are your thoughts on?

f. Look for ways to resolve problems

e.g., How can we get around this?

How about……?

What would happen if……?

Aggressive behaviour can be successful in getting us what we want. It can give us a sense of power over others and help release bad feelings, such as anger and frustration. But aggressiveness can spoil relationships, create enemies and lead to unpleasantness.

Submissive behaviour can help to defuse-a conflict very quickly by avoiding it. It helps to escape the anxiety of confrontation. But it leads to surrender of our life and aspirations to others.

But there are many more advantages to Assertive Behaviour as shown below: -

WHAT IS GOOD ABOUT BEING ASSERTIVE:

1. Assertive people are more confident, less punishing; less anxious.
2. Assertive people are more pro-active-they make

things happen.

3. Assertive people are good at focusing on real issues.
4. Assertive people are good at listening.
5. Assertive people are good at being objective — they do not jump to conclusions.
6. Assertive people are good at resolving conflicts/ complaints.
7. Assertive people are good at "Communication"; if you assert yourself in positive language with congruent non-verbal behaviour, your communication will be more effective/have more impact, whatever the purpose of your talk.
8. Assertiveness leads to better relationships with friends, society, etc... it leads to a better quality of life.
9. Assertiveness helps to maintain self-respect.
10. Assertiveness helps to avoid exploitation and manipulation.
11. Assertiveness helps to deal with fear, anger and depression.

WHY ARE WE NOT NATURALLY ASSERTIVE?

Since Assertiveness has many advantages and it would seem to be a good idea to be an assertive person, the question that crops up is "Why don't we always, naturally, assert ourselves?"

The following are some of the possible reasons why we are not naturally assertive:

a) Our Social Class: Assertiveness comes quite naturally to people with money, privilege and educational opportunities. Their background gives them a sense of self-assurance in any situation and this helps them to be assertive. Most of us do not have this self-assurance and we are apt to behave less assertively in situations we are not sure of.

b) Our Gender: Little girls are taught to defer to the wisdom of others. Little boys are allowed to assert themselves. This can result in passive behaviour in women and aggressive behaviour in men.

c) Our Schools often reward the obedient, quiet child. The inquisitive, opinion - giving child may be seen as disruptive who makes life too uncomfortable for teachers.

d) We may have learned early in life that we are praised for doing what others want us to do or punished for being "Strong-willed".

e) Our culture, our religious belief system may teach us for e.g. to "turn the other cheek" or ingrain the idea that 'the meek shall inherit the earth".

The Right to Assert Yourself

Assertiveness recognizes that individuals, no matter how imperfect, have rights. That includes you. Sometimes you may forget this and think that other people's rights are more important than yours. They are not. Remember your rights are equal to everyone else's. Therefore, claim your rights.

When you don't claim your rights, you are encouraging others to be Aggressive towards you. When you deny others their rights, you are being Aggressive towards them and are trying to force them to be submissive.

Some of the Assertive Rights are: [You will probably find others you would like to add]

1) I have the right to ask for what I want [realizing that the other person has the right to say "NO"].

2) I have the right to make my own decisions and to

cope with the consequences.

3) I have the right to make mistakes.
4) I have the right to be successful.
5) I have the right to change my mind.
6) I have the right to privacy.
7) I have the right to be alone and independent.
8) I have the right to change myself and become an Assertive person.
9) I have the right to be me.
10) I have the right to Choose.
11) I have the right to express my feelings.
12) I have the right to Disagree.
13) I have the right to be treated as an Equal.
14) I have the right to be wrong.
15) I have the right to an Opinion.
16) I have the right to say "yes' or "no" without feeling guilty.

    [Each of these rights has its concomitant / corresponding responsibility.]

To exercise your Assertive rights, you need to:

1) Know what exactly you want.
2) Say it. Articulate it. Don't keep things bottled up within yourself.
3) Say it as soon as possible. Don't delay. Don't put off. The more you delay, the more difficult it will become for you to assert yourself.
4) Be specific. Don't be vague or wishy-washy. State clearly.
5) Be and look relaxed when you are being assertive.
6) Look at the other person in the eye while

communicating.

7) Avoid laughing nervously.
8) Don't whine or be sarcastic.

ROLLING UP YOUR SLEEVES AND BECOMING ASSERTIVE.

STEP BY STEP ACTION PLAN

Step 1] Decide firmly that you want to change your behaviour and that you are willing to give whatever it takes in terms of time and effort to do so.

Step 2] Analyse your behaviour by: -

a) Answering the questions asked in the "Assertiveness Questionnaire".
b) Draw up a list of your strengths and weaknesses.
c) Whenever possible, obtain feedback from persons who are close to you and who know you well.
d) Spell out your values and beliefs. Articulate them.
e) Ascertain the reasons why you are not assertive.

Step 3] List out the different situations in the past few months when you behaved either passively or aggressively.

Step 4] Think of the dialogues that actually took place during the situations listed in step 3. Now, carefully think how any assertive person you know would have handled the situations and then rewrite the dialogues.

Step 5] Practice Progressive Relaxation Technique and mentally and physically become totally and completely relaxed. In this relaxed state, see yourself, visualize yourself behaving assertively in different situations. See yourself feeling comfortable in different situations. Pay attention to the three main components of assertive behaviour:

a) Your Voice: Your voice should be clear, audible, well-modulated and appropriately emotional.
b) Your Verbal communication: Should be well-organized, expressive, honest, clear.
c) Your non-verbal communication: Appropriate eye-contact, well-balanced posture, gestures congruent and in harmony with your verbal communication.

Step 6] Imagining and role-playing your Assertiveness: Find an understanding friend and role-play with him/her. Imagine yourself acting in an assertive manner. Behave the way you imagined yourself behaving when you were relaxed. Ask your friend to give his feedback and listen to it non-defensively. Make necessary changes and do some more role-playing till the time you feel comfortable with your new behaviour.

Step7] Select a low-risk situation in real life and practice behaving assertively. Analyse how you did and how you felt. If necessary, go back to role-playing. Keep on switching between role-playing and real-life situations until you feel quite at ease with the NEW ASSERTIVE YOU.

Always remember:

Assertiveness is not a cure-all
The ability to discern is very important while using assertiveness skills.
When two assertive persons meet they respect each other and they agree to disagree.

Assertiveness Questionnaire

Answer the following questions by placing a YES or NO. For all the YES answers, write down the reasons why.

When you apply or practice the suggestions made in this chapter in your day to day life, soon some of the YES answers will become NO.

1) Do you buy things you don't really want because you find it difficult to say "NO to the sales person?
2) When a sales person shows you things do you feel you must buy something?
3) Do you find it difficult to start a conversation with a stranger?
4) Do you find it difficult to criticize a friend?
5) Do you find it difficult to compliment a friend?
6) Do you feel self-conscious when somebody compliments you?
7) Do you find it difficult to ask a queue-breaker to join the Q?
8) Do you think you are being exploited or pushed around?
9) Do you feel dissatisfied with your social life?
10) Do you have trouble asking favours of a friend?
11) Do you get "I should have said that" kind of thoughts after social meetings?
12) Do you find it difficult to say NO to a friend even when he makes an unreasonable request?
13) Do you think that people find you boring?
14) Do you have trouble expressing your tender and angry feelings to men?
15) Do you have trouble expressing your tender and angry feelings to women?

16) Do you find it difficult to maintain eye-contact when talking to people?
17) Do you have trouble asking for an overdue increment?
18) Do you find it difficult to speak in public?
19) Do you have a fear of failure?
20) Do you feel uncomfortable when you are being watched while you are working?
21) Do you find it uncomfortable when there is a silence at a social gathering?
22) Are you afraid of making mistakes?
23) Are you always defensive when you are being criticized?
24) Do you have trouble maintaining relationships or friendships?
25) Do you feel dissatisfied with your vocation/ profession/job?
26) Do you complete other people's sentences, before they can finish saying them?
27) Are you always in a hurry?
28) Do you often lose your temper?
29) If somebody has borrowed a valuable thing from you, do you avoid asking for it, even when overdue?
30) Are you uncomfortable while contributing to a discussion or a debate?

Chapter 10

STRESS MANAGEMENT

Stress is our body's response to a difficult situation, which a person perceives as threatening. Stress is a condition caused due to mental or physical exertions, mood fluctuations, and fear about the future. It is a situation when a person is under immense mental and/or physical strain. It affects the psychological condition of a person. Stress cannot be ignored.

Stress is on the increase these days because of a variety of reasons — demanding work pressures; intense competition; compulsions to achieve targets and reach goals; having to cope with a fast-changing world; increase in crime rate which gives rise to fear which, in turn, generates stress; fast-paced city life; rapid technological changes and the struggle to keep pace with the change [having to learn new skills for example] more working mothers resulting in less time for family; too many options available for educational pursuits, career, housing, consumer goods and services, etc.

External or Internal Stress: Stress is caused by external factors or internal factors. External stressors may be physical or psychological. Physical conditions could be intense physical pain, extreme hot or cold temperatures, etc. Psychological conditions could be being trapped in an abusive relationship, poor working conditions, etc.

The internal stressors can be physical — an infection for e.g., or psychological --- an intense worry about something which may or may not occur. It seems that besides humans no other animal suffers from psychological stressors.

Acute and Chronic stress: Stressors can be acute [Short — term] or chronic [long-term].

Acute Stress: Acute stress is the reaction to a perceived imminent threat or danger for e.g. if I am afraid of dogs [and I am] and a ferocious dog suddenly and unexpectedly crosses my path, it will cause me intense stress. Some other acute stressors could be hunger, over-crowding, noise, etc. Once the acute stress passes, the person returns to normal.

Chronic Stress: There are some stressful situations which are not short-lived but are ongoing. This results in chronic stress. Some chronic stressors are prolonged illness; heavy and persistent financial problems; ongoing professional pressures, etc.

Positive Aspects of stress: Stress response can be an asset for raising levels of performance during critical events such as sports activity, an important meeting or in a situation of actual danger or crisis. Under stress, a person tends to be more focused on what he is doing; stress strengthens decision-making ability and also develops the ability to channelize restlessness. It helps to give better performance under pressure and hence this gives rise to healthy competition. Lastly, stress also induces a person to get self-activated. Appropriate and controllable stress provides interest and excitement and motivates the individual to greater achievement, while a lack of stress may lead to boredom and depression.

Negative Effects of stress: However, if stress becomes persistent, it produces physical or psychological damage over time. Chronic stress can give rise to:

a) Depression or Anxiety: Stress diminishes the quality of life by reducing feelings of pleasure and accomplishments and relationships are often threatened.

b) Cardiac disease

c) Stroke

d) Ulcers, indigestion, inflammatory bowel disease.

e) Headaches

f) Gastrointestinal problems

g) Insomnia; sleep disturbances

h) Skin allergies

Stress also gives rise to emotional problems like loss of self-esteem, lack of enthusiasm, mood swings, etc. Behaviourally, a person becomes aggressive, is unable to relax, and suffers the loss of appetite. It also results in poor work performance.

The following categories of people are more susceptible than others to suffer stress:

a) Working Women: Whether married or unmarried — bear greater and more diffused workload than men or other women.

b) People who are targets of gender or racial discrimination

c) Minority groups

d) Elderly people because of major stressors such as medical problems, financial worries, drop in living standards, loss of spouse, etc.

e) Work-Risk Factors: Some of the intense workplace stressors are:

   i. Long hours

   ii. Excessive traveling resulting in huge chunks of time spent away from home and family.

   iii. No Job-security

   iv. Unreasonable demands and relentless pressure for performance, Office politics, back-biting and conflicts between staff members

v. Responsibilities far in excess of remuneration paid.

f. Divorced or widowed individuals.

g. The unemployed, particularly those who badly need a job.

h. Isolated and lonely individuals

i. Persons, especially the retired and the elderly, who have no Health Insurance

j. Persons with no Social Network: The lack of an established network of family and friends makes one more vulnerable to stress and stress-related health problems.

k. Angry Personalities: There are persons with Type A personalities. Such persons are more predisposed to stress because they react in a very angry and hostile manner which increases stress. They tend to make a "Catastrophe" of everything thereby experiencing events and situations as more stressful than other persons.

Blue Print for Reducing Stress: Stress is an inevitable fact of life. It cannot ever be completely eliminated. One can only try to reduce or control stress. A few steps to reduce stress are:

1. **Proper Attitude:** Develop an attitude which prompts you to develop "The courage to change the things you can change, the serenity to accept the things you cannot change and the wisdom to know the difference".
2. **Self-Discipline:** Cultivate the Self-discipline which will give you the strength to have "no regrets or remorse about the past; no undue excitement about the present; and no fears and worries about the future".
3. **Keep Proper Perspective:** Always have the big picture in mind. Look at any situation in the context of your whole life. Don't over-exaggerate the importance

of any situation/event in your life.

4. **Work in your Area of Strength:** When you work in your area of strength, a difficulty or obstacle stimulates you and brings out the best in you. It challenges and motivates you. On the other hand, if you are working in your area of weakness, a difficulty or obstacle becomes threatening and stressful.
5. **Develop a Sense of Humour:** An effective way to cope with stress is to use Humour. Laughter is the best medicine. Laughter, particularly if you can laugh at yourself, helps to keep a proper perspective. It also reduces stress hormone levels.
6. **Practice Positive mind talk or self-talk:** Positive self-talk lifts our mood — it puts us in a happy frame of mind. Negative self-talk has the opposite effect. Therefore, avoid or eliminate all negative mind-talk.
7. **Establish or Strengthen a Support Network:** People who have a very good network of social support tend to remain happy and healthy despite many life stresses.
8. **Keep Pets:** Having a pet helps to reduce stress.
9. **Stay Busy:** Being engaged or occupied in meaningful work is a tremendous stress-buster.
10. **Stay away from places with bad memories:** These meaninglessly keep you stuck in the past, cause unnecessary unhappiness and increase stress.
11. **Develop a healthy lifestyle:** A Healthy diet, regular exercise, swimming, brisk walking, aerobics, stretching exercises, dancing, sports, games, etc. all help to reduce stress.
12. **Practice Yoga, Meditation, Massage Therapy:** All these are very effective in controlling or reducing stress.

13. **Add daily pleasant events:** Work to bring more pleasant events into your life. Pleasant events have very positive effects. Make time for recreation. Replace unpleasant and unnecessary chores with pleasurable or interesting activities; enjoy long weekends or frequent short vacations.
14. **Discuss your Feelings:** Talk to loved ones; open up to close friends; Don't bottle up your feelings. Learn to "Let your feelings out". Also, learn to listen, empathize and respond.
15. **Engage in Fun Activities:** Cultivate Hobbies; Watch funny movies and comedy programs; read humorous books; do crossword puzzles; Sudoku, etc.; engage in gardening; listen to music of your choice; watch or participate in sports activity.
16. **Don't be Self-Opinionated:** Don't be rigid. Don't be stubborn. Be flexible. Accept the viewpoints of others or, at least, gracefully accept that others can have different views; different perspectives. Don't adopt the "I am always right" attitude.
17. **Enjoy clean, Healthy sex:** Good sex is a tremendous stress-buster.
18. **Financial Planning:** Manage finances prudently; Plan for financial security for self and family.
19. **Learn to Live in the Present:** Don't over load your mind with regrets and remorse about the past or fears and worries about the future. These are "excess baggage" Learn to "let go".
20. **Practice Detachment:** Be a little detached. Take your work seriously but don't take yourself too seriously. Learn to laugh at yourself.
21. **Pray:** If you are a Believer and inclined to pray, then do pray. Prayer is a big coping mechanism and can relieve stress.

22. **Seek Professional Help:** If, in spite of all the above, stress still persists, then it is advisable to seek professional help in the matter.

`Chapter 11

PERSONALITY DEVELOPMENT

Personality simply means what people think of me. Do they consider me to be a nice, friendly, sociable, helpful person? Or do they look down upon me as a snob or a killjoy or someone who should be kept at arm's length? In short, my personality is what I see in the eyes of my beholders. We can say that a person has four basic aspects:

- External appearance
- Intellectual or mental capacity
- Values
- Emotional balance

Personality development means presentation. It is reflected in the way you carry yourself, the way you come across, the way you present yourself, the impact you make, and the effect you produce on others.

The first few seconds when you meet anybody or talk to anybody, are very crucial. In the first few seconds, impressions are quickly formed, and first impressions are last impressions. You never get a second chance to make a fantastic first impression.

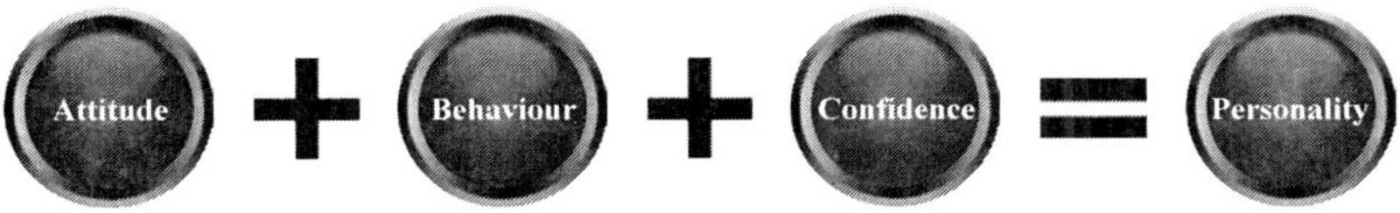

Personality is A+B+C, i.e. Attitude + Behaviour + Confidence. Personality has a lot to do with the appropriate display of energy and enthusiasm. It is analogous with colour. It shines through a smile, eye contact, handshake, body language, presentation, knowledge and intelligence.

1. Smile

Smile is a way to show willingness to serve. This requires a positive mental attitude (PMA). PMA is your focus on life, the lens with which you view the world. PMA helps you to focus on your strengths and not weaknesses; on your powers and not limitations; on capabilities and not difficulties; on opportunities and not problems; on how to get things done and not why they cannot be done.

Importance of smile

Smile increases face value. It is the most inexpensive way to improve one's looks — a free cosmetic. A smile is a positive energy force that spreads around easily. Have you ever felt the energy that exudes from a smile? It energises all those who see it. In every language, a smile means a light at the window which shows that there is a caring individual inside. A smile is the shortest distance between two people. It is a curved line that makes everything else straight and smooth. It is your passport, your ambassador, your salesperson — it opens doors of opportunity for you. A smile covers miles; it is a great icebreaker, a signal of confidence and friendliness. It is nature's way of telling someone: 'I like you.' It wordlessly conveys the message: 'I am happy to see you. I am approachable. Feel free to come and talk to me.'

A smile reduces tension and worry. We do not smile because we are happy; we are happy because we smile. A smile costs you nothing but gives you what no cosmetic on earth can give: a pleasant and forthcoming appearance. A sincere and heartfelt smile elicits a similar response, bringing pleasure to the one who smiles and to the one who receives it. Therefore, smile your way through life, for a smile is a win-win way of conquering life.

Think of all your boons and bounties. Think, thank and smile. Say 'cheese' — a little louder please! Perfect your smile by practicing it in front of a mirror. Your smile should convey confidence, not arrogance. It should exude warmth. Finally, remember that whatever else you wear, do not forget to wear a smile.

2. Eye contact

A smile does not mean anything without eye contact. Every face speaks a language of its own and eyes are an important part of speech of that language. Eye contact is important because it helps you to focus your attention on the person you are talking to. It promotes trust and confidence. It sends a non-verbal signal: 'I am attentive. I am with you. You and your message are important to me.' In summary, eye contact is an important communication tool.

3. Handshake

A handshake is the first socially acceptable physical contact. It is important to shake hands well. A good handshake has great relevance. It reflects a confident personality. Your handshake should be firm, confident, accompanied by a smile and eye contact. Do not open palms, do not have a weak handshake. At the same time, the grip should not be too firm —

it certainly cannot be bone-crushing. Avoid a double-handed handshake in the corporate context.

4. Body language

It is important to display good body language. A good posture suggests that you are paying attention. Do not slouch, lean or place your elbows on the table while in a meeting. Your body language should convey and transmit vibrancy, energy, enthusiasm, willingness and readiness to act, to serve, to take charge. In short, always be in a 'ready' position.

A Few Tips

While standing

- Stand tall
- Do not seek physical support by holding or leaning against anything such as a wall, desk, board, table, chair, etc.
- Appear neither arrogant nor diffident, i.e., do not tilt your head up or down — keep it level
- Keep your hand close to your body or at waist level in the 'terminus' position with your palms loosely held in front of your chest
- Do not put hands in your pockets; also, do not cross your arms in front of you or at the back.

While sitting

- Sit straight on the chair
- Sit slightly leaning forward
- Avoid resting your back on the backrest when in a meeting
- Keep your hand on your lap or on the edge of the table
- Keep your feet on the floor, close together
- Keep your head level— appearing neither diffident nor arrogant

While walking

- Move purposefully with rhythm, energy and enthusiasm
- Do not drag your feet
- Keep your head level

5. Presentation

Personality is gauged by the right display of energy and enthusiasm. It lends colour to the way you present yourself. The three important factors in an individual's presentation are:

- Verbal (7%)
- Vocal (38%)
- Visual (55%)

(Percentage scores indicate the impact of each factor; borrowed from research by Albert Mehrabian.)

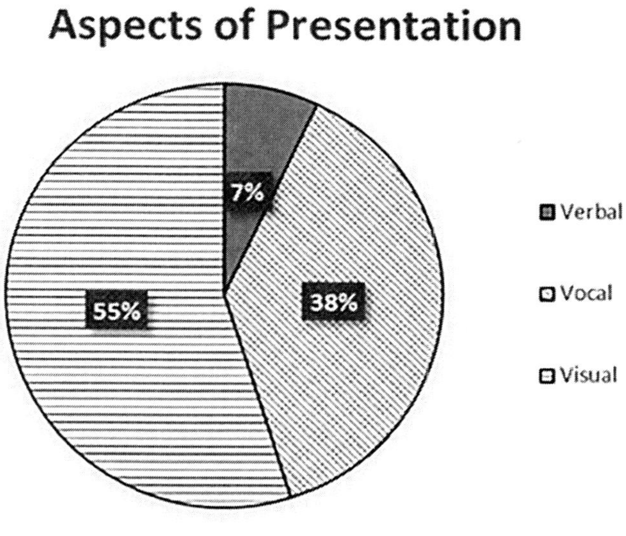

Always keep these three factors and their relative importance in mind during your communication/presentation.

6. Knowledge/Intelligence

It is not enough to only make a good first impression. It is important to sustain it. The style will open the door of opportunity for you, but substance and sincerity are what keep it open. Therefore, develop knowledge and substance. Intelligence is a combination of collection and production of knowledge. The Internet has opened up multiple avenues to gather knowledge, ideas and opinions, apart from newspapers and magazines. Garner knowledge about global affairs. Also, strive to develop a global personality. Widen your horizons. It is very important to have knowledge and opinions on various issues. Use a mix of the Internet, radio, television, print media, etc. to develop your personality.

Communication and Personality

In communication, linkage is important. Therefore, in a conversation, shift to different topics only after establishing some link. While speaking, speak with some emotion, connection and heart. Share intriguing, fascinating facts.

Avoid saying 'no', especially in sales and service. Instead, say: 'Let me look that up for you' — and genuinely try to find an alternative. Say, 'I am willing to try/learn.' Do not use abbreviations in conversations. Avoid slang and never use foul language.

Be dignified

Be poised, carry yourself well. Do not be pedestrian or run-of-the-mill. You are special. You are important. Be a trendsetter, not a follower.

Bring authenticity in your communication

Do not be vague and ambiguous. Give documentary evidence, statistics or facts when needed. Quote sources of facts or information. Talk with examples and illustrations while explaining an idea or concept to another. An effective presentation is synonymous with increase in believability. While making conversations, do not be abrupt. Give impressive descriptions —something that will intrigue, fascinate and enamour the listener. Be simple and natural in communication. Do not put on a fake accent — it does not impress anyone. Avoid incorrect language. Do not fidget or scratch while talking and avoid fillers. Smile — it will carry you far and long.

Enrich your word power

The moment you read or hear a new word, use it a few times in your social intercourse. Read with a pencil or pen in hand (use the highlighter in case of an e-book) and mark the words you do not understand. Look them up in a dictionary as soon as possible. Start using that word in your conversations and written work such as emails. Learn to pronounce words correctly and enunciate clearly.

Learn public speaking

Public speaking is a tremendous confidence booster. Speak or create opportunities to speak in public — at weddings, fetes, social functions, college events, etc. Compere shows — all this will enhance your personality.

Never let your status come in the way

Sell newspapers/magazines, sing, be a waiter, do telemarketing, work in a call centre, engage in multi¬level marketing and networking — especially when you are young. The experience will always enrich you.

Do everything to enhance your personality

Expose yourself to different situations: call up five-star hotels to make enquiries; respond to advertisements; help in organising fests/fairs; take up jobs in fast food chains, retail outlets, work in a library, etc. These opportunities help you face customers and meet good people along the way. For enhancing your personality, it is important to meet with different people and discuss issues. Be actively involved in social/community events. Join organizations such as Rotaract or Toastmasters clubs that provide umpteen opportunities for public speaking and leadership development.

Dress sense

Always be appropriately dressed for the occasion. Take care of your grooming and personal hygiene—look good, smell good.

Courtesy

Always be courteous; use courtesy words liberally. The three most important words in manners/etiquette are:

- Thank you
- Sorry
- Please

Use these three and other courtesy words often and appropriately. Never speak to a person in a language he does not understand. It is extremely rude to do so. Likewise, when in a group, ensure that the conversation is carried on in a language which everyone understands. An aspect of courtesy is the ability to take pleasantly, in your stride, the discourteous behaviour of others. In fact, the essence of good manners is to be able to put up with a person of bad manners. Finally, keep in mind the famous words of Abraham Lincoln: "I am courteous with him not because he is a gentleman, but because I am a gentleman."

Charm

Develop a charming personality. Be warm and sensitive. Develop listening skills and a sense of humour. Inculcate empathy in your character and bring charm to your conversation. The ability to compliment another makes a person charming. Be sincere and sound sincere when you compliment; learn the art of complimenting. The desire and ability to compliment well reflects a personality that keeps its eyes and ears open to the 'good' in the things/persons around him; therefore, practice complimenting. Give at least 3-5 compliments every day. They improve the quality of your personal, social as well as work life. However, do not overdo it or indulge in cheap flattery.

Values

A good personality is built on the foundation of a sound value system. What are values and how do they figure in the development of personality? Values are what we hold as right or wrong, fair and unfair, good and bad. Values may be legal, i.e. what the law prescribes as right or wrong; they may also be religious, i.e. a religion lays down actions as correct or incorrect, moral or immoral, etc. In our quest for personality development, we do not concern ourselves with legal or religious values. What we are concerned with here are social values. For example:

- Will you buy a movie ticket in the black market?
- Will you buy a pirated book or a CD?
- Will you bribe a policeman when you are caught breaking traffic rules?

There are some simple tests to find out whether a particular matter relates to a value or not. According to Shiv Khera (in his book 'You Can Win'), one such test is whether you would do a certain thing if your children are around.

Emotional Balance

Human beings are pulled and pushed by reason on the one hand and emotions on the other. Often, we find ourselves overpowered by strong emotions such as love, hatred, fear, worry, shame, etc. Emotions have the power of overpowering reason and thought. We see this happening in many instances in our lives. A good, well-developed personality must not be unduly swayed by emotions and must be able to strike a balance between reasons and emotions. This is also called Emotional Quotient (EQ). An aspect of personality development is acquiring a high EQ.

Chapter 12

ALL ABOUT COMMUNICATION

Communication is derived from the Latin word 'communus', which means common ground: To make common, to transmit, to impart... It implies sharing and interaction and both of these are very important for communication.

Communication is central to everything in life. Almost all problems can be linked to communication. All living beings communicate. Communication is so important and pervasive that American President Calvin Coolidge said, "If we improve our communication by 10%, the world will improve by 60%."

Types of communication

Basically, there are two types of communication: Verbal (where words are used) and non-verbal (words are not used).

Verbal communication can be oral or written. Non-verbal communication would include communication by:

- Signals, such as traffic signals, hand movements indicating come, go, wave, etc.
- Symbols, such as sporting black bands in protest, wearing a ring to indicate marriage, etc.
- Silence, which can communicate fear, respect, contempt, etc.

- Touch, such as a push, kick, handshake, hug, holding hands, etc.
- Smile, which usually indicates that you like somebody or that you are happy, friendly, etc.
- Eye-contact, which shows a person is truthful, confident. Lack of eye contact conveys lack of confidence, non-transparency, deceit.
- Facial expressions that convey joy, sorrow, optimism, pessimism, etc.
- Gestures and posture may show comfort or lack of it, friendliness or hostility, confidence or shyness, etc.
- Vocal paralanguage may convey anger, sarcasm, affection, etc.

Non-verbal communication is more important than verbal communication. The components of communication, according to Albert Mehrabian's oft-quoted study are:

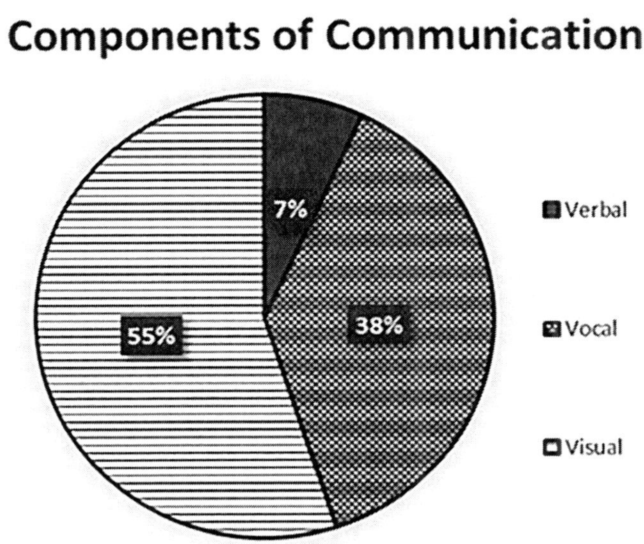

it or not. Here's a story: In an exclusive primary school, the rule was that students will not carry any pens/pencils/books from home. Everything was provided by the school. In the morning, the students would receive the books, pencils, etc. and at the end of the day, they would return them to the teachers. One day, on counting, a teacher found that she was one pencil short. She kept quiet. The next day, the same thing happened. This went on for a few days. The teacher did not carry out any search. However, one day, she caught a student hiding a pencil in her clothes.

The student was taken to the Principal where she confessed that every day, she was taking a pencil home. The Principal did not want to punish or rebuke the child. Instead, she rang up the child's father, who was the CEO of a multi-national corporation. The Principal told the father, "I am sorry to inform you that your child is taking home pencils from the school." The father immediately snapped and said, "My child is taking pencils from the school! Why should she do this? Every day I bring home lovely pencils from my office for her."

The CEO did not realize that every day, he was communicating to the child that it is ok to bring home pencils not belonging to him. So, the child reasoned that it was ok for her to take home pencils belonging to the school.

Difference between 'Efficient' and `Effective' communication

Efficient communication is good communication. It is when the message is communicated clearly, completely and without any distortion. What the sender says and what the receiver understands are the same.

Effective communication is more than efficient communication. When the communication is good and also the 'desired action' results, then the communication is effective. This requires elements of persuasion, motivation, and sometimes even force.

In order to be effective in communication, it is vital that

there should be congruence between verbal and non-verbal communication. Otherwise, the listener will either be confused or listen to non-verbal communication.

Perception is very important. It is not what the sender says but what the receiver hears that is important. The parents may be expressing love, care and concern when they ask their teenaged daughter about her coming home late, but the daughter 'hears' interference, nagging, lack of trust, etc. and communication breaks down.

Another important aspect of effective communication is feedback. If there is trust (without which effective communication is not possible), between the sender and receiver, honest, objective feedback can be sought or given.

Semantics is important because words mean different things to different people. In order to ensure that there is no communication gap, care must be taken to see that all parties in a communication event understand keywords in one and the same sense.

Some obstacles to effective communication are:

- Fear: If there is fear of consequences, communication will not be honest and hence it will be ineffective.
- Egos of the persons communicating
- Shyness on the part of one or both the parties
- Low self-image will prevent effective communication
- Operating out of past experiences (pre-conceived notions) is a big obstacle to effective communication

In addition, there are certain other traits that render communication ineffective, chief of which are:

- Certification: almost all people indulge in it
- Clarification: Seeking or giving clarification is mainly done by young people
- Repetition: Old people often do this
- Justification: Unhappy people tend to do this

Barriers to communication

- Physical barriers: Noise, heat, poor reception of signals, mechanical breakdowns, etc.
- Semantic barriers: Different understanding of words among people
- If the sender and receiver attribute different meanings to the same word, communication fails. We may here quote the classic example of a senior manager telling a new assistant, "Take this important document to the stockroom and torch it (i.e. make a copy of it on a machine which is operated by a heat process). The new assistant was puzzled but was afraid to ask questions, so he burned the document with a lighted match.
- Attitudes and opinions: We react favourably or are hostile depending on whether the information being transmitted is to our personal advantage or not.
- Our emotions: We can neither receive nor transmit message effectively if we are under the grip of strong emotions such as anger, hatred, jealousy, etc.
- Status consciousness: If we are over-conscious of our lower or higher rank, we are unable to express ourselves candidly.
- Source of communication: We react according to the trust we repose in the source from which the communication emanates.
- Inattentiveness: Unconsciously, we become inattentive if the communication contains a new idea and our mind refuses to respond to it.
- Unsolicited communication: We are unresponsive if the communication is unsolicited (such as an unsolicited sales letter, advice, etc.).

Communication and Inter-personal relations

Words can build up relationships. We can use communication to build good relationships. Some of the things we can do are:

- Appreciate people: Give sincere appreciation generously. Being appreciated is one of our deepest desires. It makes a person feel important. Develop a wardrobe of vocabulary and use it to praise people.
- Acknowledge people: Acknowledge people for what they have done. Thank sincerely and meaningfully. Thank enthusiastically, politely and courteously.
- Admit mistakes: Say sorry; have no ego hassles.
- Smile: Smile big and often.
- Avoid arguments: You can never win an argument; even if you win, you lose.
- Always be courteous and polite: Show consideration/ sensitivity. Use courtesy words as often as possible. Small courtesies will improve relationships.
- Do not gossip.
- Use the following and similar sentences as frequently as possible:
    - Thank you very much
    - I am sorry, please forgive me
    - Let me help you/I would like to help you
    - You look great/terrific
    - I am so proud of you
    - I missed you so much
    - How sweet is your child!
    - Go ahead, I am with you
    - Let's go out for lunch/dinner (to acknowledge

good work done)

- o I love you very much

Essentials of effective oral communication

- Clear pronunciation
- Brevity: Be brief without sacrificing clarity, courtesy and completeness. Do not overload the receiver with irrelevant details.
- Precision: Be precise and not vague. For example, instead of saying 'I will come early tomorrow', say, 'I will come at 9 a.m. tomorrow!'
- Conviction: If the sender has conviction about his message, he will be more effective.
- Logical sequence: The message should be given in a proper order and not haphazardly.
- Appropriate word choice: Exercise care in the choice of words used.
- Avoid waffle words: Do not litter your communication with waffle or weasel words such as all', 'uhm', 'you see', 'you know', 'ok', etc.
- Natural voice: Speak in your natural voice. Do not put on an accent or try to imitate somebody.
- Right register: Keep the listener in mind. After all, it is not what you say, but what he/she 'hears' that matters.

A few hints to make your oral communication more effective

- Use simple, clear, concise and accurate language.
- Carefully watch the listener's face while delivering the message to make sure that the message is getting through.

- Give the receiver the opportunity to ask questions. In fact, if he is shy or fearful, encourage him, prompt her to ask questions so that it is ensured that the message is understood (and later acted upon) correctly.
- Repeat complicated instructions.
- Do not assume that the listener has prior knowledge of the topic of communication. Seek clarification on this score.
- Organise your instruction logically, sequentially, chronologically, etc.

Importance of humour in communication/conversation

- Humour is saline to life.
- Humour reduces tension, it eases situations and makes others happy.
- You can point out defects without hurting others.
- Smile and laughter increase-life span.
- A square mouth reduces life span.
- Humour is a good icebreaker.
- Humour diffuses volatile situations.
- Humour adds spark to conversation.
- Humour results in more openness. People loosen up and drop their masks.
- Humour must be relevant.
- Humour is always welcome in conversation and sometimes even critically needed.
- A cardinal rule in speech and conversation is never stay serious for too long'.
- But humour, like anything else, does not work if it is forced. It is a turn off if it is forced. Whatever your style of humour, let it come into the conversation naturally —just be yourself.

- Bringing everything to a halt so that you can tell your gag is bad timing. Do not interrupt a conversation in progress just so you can tell a joke you heard.
- Purpose of humour is to entertain, to provide relief. While doing that, please ensure that your joke is relevant and appropriate and that it is not vulgar or offensive, and that it is not against any religion or caste. If you can cut jokes on yourself, people will love you for that.
- Humour is an essential means of communication and influence. It is very effective and relevant to workplace issues such as communication, group dynamics and conflict management.
- Humour is a social lubricant, with regard to its role in communication. We like people who make us laugh. Therefore, it plays a valuable role in group harmony and in communication systems. It is a relatively safe way of raising risky issues.
- Humour is also an aid in communication in teaching and learning situations. When used effectively, it can support understanding and retention of information and can assist in establishing rapport.
- Humour makes significant contribution to the effectiveness of a group. Among the many potential benefits of humour in group situations are, more open, less defensive communication, greater group cohesiveness and feelings of belonging. Humour also helps to reduce tension and boredom.
- Laughter can effectively relieve tension in conflict situations. A well-timed joke can refocus negotiation in a more positive direction-it helps people re-think their approaches. It is impossible to laugh heartily and be angry at the same time. Humour helps in alleviating hostile attitudes.

- Use of humour is a potentially ‘high risk, high payoff intervention. It is especially helpful to use oneself as the target of humour.

Guidelines for effective use of humour

- Start with yourself: “You grow up the day you have your first laugh at yourself.”
- Take your work seriously, but yourself lightly: You can thus perceive and appreciate the humour in every day encounters.
- Be an observer: Be aware that you are surrounded by humour and notice it. For example, you can find it in signs that are displayed, in typographical errors and in slips of the tongue.
- Use humour as a support for competence rather than as a means of masking a lack of it.
- Use humour with sensitivity and care so that it is likely to be appreciated.

We can conclude this chapter by saying that one should always maintain dignity and decorum, always communicate with courtesy and respect, should display our class in communication by talking with style. We should ‘stand out’ through our communication. After all, you are not another ordinary person on the street; so, do not be pedestrian. Do not be run-of-the-mill. Always remember: “Without effective communication, skill is an uncut diamond.”

Chapter 13

COMMUNICATION & TRANSACTIONAL ANALYSIS [T.A]

According to T.A, everyone's personality has 3 parts, called ego states. These ego states are named Parent; Adult and Child. When we capitalize these words, we are talking about ego states rather than real parents, adults and children. TA seeks to explain all inter-personal human behaviour as transactions out of these ego states of interacting individuals. TA is a way of understanding human behaviour.

It has been established that to think of the brain as a video-recorder with both a record and play-back function is a fair comparison. It is believed that all our experiences throughout life are recorded in our brains and can be played back at any time in response to the right stimulus. Each person is made up of several different "egos" - we can think of each ego as a different tape. Each person is thought of as a combination of 3 tapes: -

1. Parent Tape: Contains recordings of prejudices as well as helpfulness.
2. Adult Tape: Contains recordings of facts and common sense.
3. Child Tape: Contains recording of feelings — happy and unreasonable ones.

Every person contains all 3 types of tapes. They are equally good, have strong and weak points and can be appropriate under different circumstances. They are, however, unlikely to be of equal size and the balance between the 3 make up each individual's personality: T.A is a way of understanding behaviour based on the belief that we can learn from studying more closely the way our decisions and communications are based on our thoughts and feelings.

Parent Ego State: The basic information on this tape comes from our experiences of life with parents / teachers in early life — "Sit up straight at Table" — "Use knife and Fork" ....

Everyone develops a parent ego state when as children they absorb certain attitudes and ways of behaving from parental figures. When you feel, think, or act as you saw your parents [or other authority figures] act when you were little, you are in your parent ego state — you are playing your parent tape. Parent Ego is very strongly imprinted on the brain and works automatically, particularly if we are involved in any critical or evaluation process. For this reason, we often use the phrase "Parent Tapes" to refer to:

a) Dialogue from parent figures stored in our heads, and

b) Automatic responses we make while in our parent ego state.

Sometimes parents treat their children in a loving way, speak to them, offer shelter and protection, or take care of them in other ways. We call this nurturing behaviour. If it is nourishing, it helps children grow.

At other times, parents criticize, make rules, give commands, or punish their children. Since the main objective of these behaviours is to control the child, we call them controlling behaviours.

Thus P.E has 2 sides: -

a) Controlling, Disciplining, Restricting parent. This is called the critical or the Controlling Parent. [C.P]

b) Helpful; Caring, Loving, Nurturing parent. This is called the Nurturing Parent [NP].

The Controlling Parent's words and Phrases are: -

Right — Wrong	what will people say
Good — Bad	That's the limit
Never — Always	You must never
	Why haven't you

The caring Parent's Words and Phrases are: -

Take care	Don't be afraid
I'll help you	It Won't take me long
Please remember to	Don't be late

We give below an example of the statements you are likely to make while in your parent ego:

Controlling Parent: "Nobody can leave until this report is finished."

Nurturing Parent: "I am sorry you are not feeling well today. Would you like to go over to the Doctor and get some help? I'll take care of your work.

The Controlling Parent scolds when children are late for dinner and the Caring parent is the one who is happy they arrived home safely.

Adult Ego: All facts, logical and linked experiences are recorded on your Adult Tape. Although we respond automatically when in our parent ego mode, we respond analytically when in our Adult mode. Whenever you are gathering information, reasoning things out, estimating probabilities, and so on, you are in your Adult Ego state. While in this state you are cool and collected; you make decisions unemotionally. You just want the facts. Adult Ego is the maturing and deliberating part of personality — your actions and words are sensible and well-considered. A.E collects information, tackles and solves problems in a logical, calm, collected way. You concentrate on facts, not feelings and prejudices.

As a rule, Adult Ego asks questions and seeks out facts e.g.

What is that? What do you think? Why did it happen? What are the choices / options?

Let's find out. Let's define it. How can we handle it best?

Child Ego represents the child you once were. On it are recorded all your emotions. All your early experiences, together with your initial views of yourself and others. The child Ego reacts emotionally to the feelings and instincts of childhood.

According to T.A theory, the child Ego state has 3 facets.

a) Natural Child

b) Adapted Child

c) Little Professor

The Natural Child is primitive; impulsive, instinctive, undisciplined, demanding. It is spontaneous, energetic, curious, loving, uninhibited. It's the part of us that feels free and loves pleasure. When you are in your Natural Child, you transact freely and openly with others. The natural child is the ego state you came into the world with as a newborn baby. It's what comes naturally. The natural child isn't entirely without fault, however. It can be self-centred, impatient and greedy.

In contrast, the Adapted Child acts in patterns learned from the environment. Your Adapted Child developed when you learned to change [adapt] your feelings and behaviours in response to the world around you. It carries the influence of a person's upbringing, which is 'do as you are told". It is through adaptations that we originally become socialized — able to co-operate with others and live in groups. Through socialization we learn to take turns, to share, to be friendly, to be concerned about how something feels to others. We must learn these valuable skills to get along socially. It is our Adapted Child that says "Please" and "Thank You" to customers.

The Little Professor is the "thinking" part of the child — thinking without knowing all of the facts believed to be needed. It is creative, intuitive and manipulative. With the Little Professor, a child psyches out a situation and seems to have an inborn ability to intuitively sense what to do or how to solve a problem.

Examples of Phrases in Child Ego state are: -

I like; I won't; I feel; I must; You always try to...Let's play..., Help me......

WOW! I will in a moment; if only If she can, so can I......., It's mine; etc.....

All the 3 Ego states [Parents, Adult, Child] are independent of age.

The crux of T.A as far as communication is concerned is "Have a better understanding of which tapes people are playing so that you can respond accordingly and thereby achieve smoother communication".

When under pressure, we tend to play the tape we have used most often before in a similar situation. The reaction is often spontaneous, and we do not allow ourselves time to think whether the tape is suitable or not. The 3 tapes are not of equal size. The strength of a tape depends on its frequency of use. It is this strength together with the composition of the tapes that is unique to each person.

TRANSACTIONS

Any form of Communication can be called a Transaction --- words, voice and body language. When 2 persons get together, each with a personal set of tape recordings, a transaction starts which can be observed and discussed. This is called Transactional Analysis. You can have "Parallel" or "Complementary" transactions which proceed smoothly. However, when conflict arises, the Transaction is "Crossed".

"Concealed" Transaction is when a person may appear to be playing one tape quite openly but is doing it for a different, hidden purpose.

Parallel Transactions [Complementary Transactions] occur when a person (A) communicates with a person (B) and (B) plays a tape (A) expected to be used. Parallel Transaction may occur using any of the P.A.C Tapes. In parallel Transactions, lines of communication are open, and people can continue transacting with one another.

Example of Parallel Transaction:

Man, to his wife:
"Have you seen my cufflinks?"
Wife: "Yes, I think they are in the top drawer."

Crossed Transactions occur when a person

A. Communicates a message to a person

and

B. Plays a different tape in reply to the one (A) had expected.

E.g. of Crossed Transaction:

Man, to his Wife: "Have you seen my cuff links"?

Reply of wife: "Do I always have to remember everything for you"?

In crossed transaction, people feel discounted and misunderstood.

Concealed Transaction is more complicated. They involve 2 or more ego-states at once. A hidden message is sent under the guise of a simple, socially acceptable message.

It is saying one thing and meaning another.
E.g. of Concealed Transaction:
Spouse writing with his fingers in the dust on the table
"I Love You"
[Hidden message: "The table needs dusting".]
How to maintain Adult to Adult Communication

A Quick Check List

1. Ask Open-ended Questions: e.g. "What more can you

tell me about this"?

"What other angle is there?"

"What seems to be the biggest problem"?

2. Ask Specific Questions: How did the situation arise? Who is responsible? When did it happen? How did it happen?
3. Show Understanding of Other people's feelings:

   e.g. a] You are really upset about this, aren't you?

   b] I can see this has worried you greatly.

   c] It is obvious why you are upset
4. Ask for a Clear explanation: a. Could you tell me exactly what it was...? b. Could you put it another way?
5. Listen Attentively.
6. Admit it openly if you are mistaken [This is one of the most precious assets of an adult — ego]

   e.g.: a] You are right. I got it wrong.

   b] That's quite correct, I should have

   c] Here is my mistake.
7. Check the facts: e.g. a] Are the figures correct? b] Where did you get this information? c] Is it up to date?
8. Leave open the chance of other Courses: e.g. a] Perhaps we could do it another way; b] Is this the only option?

Chapter 14

STROKES

The Importance of Attention: Strokes are any kind of attention you can get from or give to another person. Strokes are very essential for a relaxed and happy life. For people, whose basic human needs like food, shelter, clothing, etc. are met, Strokes are the greatest human need. An absence of sufficient attention can lead to a lack of competence, unusual behaviour, a loser attitude and mental disease.

The exchange of strokes between you and the people close to you is of the highest importance to your relationships: This is very poignantly and touchingly brought out in the following verse written by a 9-year-old girl:

"If you touch me soft and gentle
If you look at me and smile at me
If you listen to me talk some time before you talk
I will grow, really grow"

Categories of Strokes: There are 3 categories of strokes:

a) Positive or Negative
b) Physical or Mental
c) Conditional or Unconditional

Positive Strokes are good. They make you feel happy and useful. They give you a real boost.

Negative Strokes are bad news. They make you feel sad and downcast. They make you feel like a loser.

But No Stroke at all is worst.

Positive Strokes can be physical like a hand-shake, a pat on the back, a caress, an embrace, a kiss etc.

Positive strokes can also be mental like praise, thanks, interest, appreciation, admiration, a promotion ,etc.

Examples of Physical Negative strokes are a push, a punch, a slap, a kick, etc.

Examples of Mental Negative strokes are Criticism; sneer; Shrug; Scornful look; a turned back; being ignored, etc.

Physical Strokes: How do you make use of positive physical strokes?

At Home:

a) Give children enough hugs, kisses, cuddles.

b) Show enough tenderness and warmth towards your partner.

At Work: Give more people a hand-shake, a friendly squeeze on the arm or a light touch. It is important that the physical contact [at home or work] is made in a totally natural way. It should not be reduced to mere routine. Care should also be taken to ensure that physical contact does not degenerate into "pawing", "groping`' or "Sexual harassment". It should also be borne in mind that different countries / cultures have different degrees [of acceptability] of physical contact.

Conditional & Unconditional strokes: Strokes, whether positive, negative, physical or mental, can be conditional or unconditional.

Conditional strokes come in response to special occasions or performances. They are not a surprise. They are planned and expected for e.g. Christmas cards, Birthday presents, pocket money, etc.

Unconditional strokes are spontaneous and unpredictable. They are, therefore, more fun, stronger and warmer.

E.g.

a. Unexpected letter/phone call

b. Shout of joy from children when parent comes home

c. A mild, little flirtation.

Importance of Strokes and Stroke Balance: - Stroke Balance is like a Bank Pass Book with a debit and credit side. The difference between plus/credit/positive strokes and minus/debit/negative strokes gives you a stroke balance. If you have a debit balance, you will be a loser. If you have a credit balance, you will be a winner.

Life has been described as a battle to get strokes. This is the light that makes life worth living. It gives purpose and meaning to life. In this battle, dogs and children are most successful because they ask for attention whereas Adults do not.

Good strokes humanize and improve the quality of work life. People need strokes for their sense of survival and well-being on the job. In fact, strokes are a basic unit of motivation. As a general guide:

a) The quantity and quality of strokes serve as either positive or negative motivation for employees.

b) A good share of the satisfaction people get from work depends on the strokes available from other people.

c) We can get strokes from the activity of work itself — especially if what we are doing really “fits” and we can take responsibility for it.

For positive results on the job, it’s crucial to give people positive strokes. Therefore, an organization must set up a system whereby employees are able to get a lot of positive strokes.

3 simple rules for stroking:

- Avoid Stroking undesirable behaviour: - Typically, in an organization, people who do a good job don’t get stroked, but people who goof up get lots of attention.

This tendency tends to perpetuate mediocrity because what you stroke is what you get. Following this principle, one should avoid stroking a person for undesirable behaviour. Instead, we should think of the positive behaviour we want and stroke it.

- Time your Strokes: - In addition to staying positive, it's also important to time your strokes carefully. To be most effective in motivating a person, a stroke should come as soon as possible after a desirable performance. If the act of stroking is delayed/ postponed, the effectiveness of the stroke will be greatly reduced.
- Stroke Approximations: - It is usually a good idea to stroke positively for slight approximations of the final desired performances we expect. By "approximation" we mean a behaviour [or result of behaviour] that is approaching a desired standard. For example, when an infant flails its arms in the direction of a rattle, it is making an approximation of grasping the rattle. Similarly, the cooing and gurgling of a 3-month-old is an approximation of the animated speech that may happen at the age of two. The parents have wisely stroked these attempts. If our parents had waited for us to talk fluently before they stroked us, we would probably still be babbling, gurgling and cooing. The important point here is that it is often vital to stroke approximations. Instead of waiting for perfect or near-perfect performance, we can all motivate people by stroking them for successive approximation, each of which comes closer to our desired standard performance.

Chapter 15

DEVELOPING CONVERSATIONAL SKILLS

One of the greatest sources of joy and the greatest pleasure in life for human beings is being engaged in delightful conversation. Talking is the most essential form of communication and it distinguishes mankind from other species.

Talk is very natural for human beings. On an average, a human being speaks about 15,000 to 18,000 words per day. Since we indulge in this activity so hugely, it makes sense that we develop our conversational skills and become excellent talkers. Good talking is a skill and like all skills, it can be learned and developed. And like all skills, the more you do it, the more you practice, the better you get at it and as you get more skilled, the more you enjoy talking. You need to work hard at developing conversational skills. But it is imperative to understand the pre-requisites, the basics, first.

These are the pre-requisites for developing conversational skills:

The right attitude

The desire and the determination to talk even when you feel uncomfortable is an essential pre¬requisite to become a better conversationalist.

- Like in public speaking, you must snatch every opportunity to talk. Even if you feel embarrassed, talk out loudly to yourself. Stand in front of a mirror and talk to yourself. Look at your reflection and talk. This will also help to develop eye contact.
- Another simple technique is to talk to an infant or a pet. This is a great way to develop confidence in talking to others. And the best part is that the baby or the pet are good listeners and they will not interrupt you.

Be open

Be willing to share information. Talk about your likes and dislikes, your failures and successes, your background, your dreams, your hobbies, etc. Be open, transparent, honest and generous in revealing yourself to the others just as you would want them to share with you about themselves.

Overcome shyness

Maybe, you will feel shy to talk to someone for the first time. Do not let that deter you. Overcome your shyness. A good way to overcome shyness is to remember that we are all human beings — that the person you are talking to also puts on his pants one leg at a time. Thus, there is no need to feel shy or be afraid.

Secondly, remind yourself that the person with whom you are engaged is, more than likely, as shy as you are, perhaps even more.

It is important that you put yourself at ease and make the person also feel at ease. If you come across as a person who is enjoying the conversation, the person you are talking to will also enjoy it.

Characteristics of good conversationalists

- They have a sense of humour: And they do not hesitate to use humour on themselves. They do make fun of themselves. In fact, some of the best talkers often tell stories about themselves.
- They have their own way of talking: They have their own style. They do not try to copy or imitate or ape anyone else. They are their natural selves.
- They have broad horizons: They are well-read and well-informed. They are interested in a variety of subjects and issues and can talk easily and knowingly on a wide range of topics.
- They are different: They have the capacity to look at things from different perspectives, from new angles. Their originality is refreshing. They are able to throw new light even on mundane, familiar issues or events.
- They are inquisitive: They are curious. They genuinely want to know more about what people are telling. They frequently ask 'why?' They ask open-ended questions.
- They are empathetic: They empathize - they put themselves in the shoes of the other person. They see things from the other person's point of view and thereby relate better to what you are saying.
- They are enthusiastic: They are passionate about their lives and they are enthusiastically interested in what you are telling them at the moment.
- They are good listeners.
- They do not monopolise the conversation: Although they are open and generously share information/view/ ideas, they do not talk about themselves all the time nor do they try to dominate the conversation.

If you wish to be a good conversationalist, learn to listen. To be a good talker, you must listen well. People often do not listen. Respect begets respect. If you listen well and show people you talk to that you are interested in what they are saying, they will respond in the same way when you talk. Good listening will also help you to ask relevant and pertinent questions. Asking good follow-up questions is the hallmark of a good conversationalist.

Avoid asking close-ended (yes/no) questions. They scuttle and kill good conversation. The answer to such questions is normally only in one or two words. Asking such questions is the nemesis of a good conversation. Therefore, ask open-ended questions. They give rise to expanded answers which enliven the flow of a conversation.

Be interested in people and they will find you more interesting. People are much more interested in what is happening in their lives and their needs and challenges that they are interested in you and your problems. Therefore, encourage and stimulate people to talk about themselves and their achievements. They will enjoy talking to you about them. In other words, "to be interesting, be interested."

Body language

Body language is the natural accompaniment of speech. Let your body language be natural. It will enhance the effectiveness of your conversation. If you try to imitate others or copy others' gestures, postures, voice, etc., you may come across as insincere and fake. Be natural. Speak from the heart. Concentrate on how well you are talking, and your body language will take care of itself. Most of your body language will follow your talk easily, naturally and effortlessly. For example, you may nod your head to show agreement or shake it to express surprise or sympathy. You may also lean forward towards the person you are talking to, to stress that you are focusing on them and are hugely interested in what they are saying.

Eye contact

One rule which must never be broken is: Always maintain eye contact. This will certainly help you to become a successful talker in every situation and with everybody.

Keeping abreast

In today's fast-paced world with immense technological advances, there is a huge spurt in availability of information. People know a lot about what is happening. Moreover, they know it almost immediately. In this scenario, to be an effective conversationalist, it is essential to keep abreast of what is going on in people's mind and what they are dealing with. In other words, you have to be relevant if you wish to be a success in your social conversations.

Opening a conversation

For any situation — a party, a dinner, calling on new neighbours, etc. — there are many safe subjects with which you can open a conversation, especially if you know the person well. If not, you can always talk about a current sporting event, hobbies, weather, pets, children, etc. Sometimes, the occasion itself can become a good starting point. At a get-together in somebody's house or office, you may find artefacts, paintings, pictures, mementos, photographs, etc. which can provide a safe subject for beginning a conversation. And your host will certainly love to talk about them.

Getting out of a conversation

When you feel you have had enough of a person or a

group and would now like to move on, you can do this very graciously and politely. You can make your exit using any one of the following excuses:

"This food is yummy. I think I will go and get a second helping."

"Excuse me; I need to visit the rest room."

"Please excuse me, I would like to go and see our host."

"Mr. X, have you met Mr. Y... (Introduce them to each other) ... I'll be back in a moment while you two carry on."

"Excuse me, let me go and mingle with some others."

"It was nice talking to you."

Making your exit is no big deal. So, do not read too much into it or make too much of it. Just wait for a slight pause in the conversation, say something polite and move on as if it is a natural thing to do.

Social occasions vary from small get-togethers to huge events, big weddings, etc. The principles of conversation are the same. Be open, find the common ground with your partner and always listen.

An important thing which one must always keep in mind is that the secret of a good conversation is 'asking questions'. And one of the most provocative questions is 'why?' It is one of the best questions to keep the conversation flowing and make it exciting and interesting.

Suggestions to make parties more enjoyable

- Make sure that the conversation is carried on in a language which all present can understand. Talking in a language which people do not understand is not only a social gaffe but also very rude.
- Likewise, choose or keep the conversation going on a topic in which everyone is interested. Avoid topics

that only some of the guests are interested in or have knowledge about.

- Seek opinions. Do not try to impose your opinions on others. You will be a better conversationalist if you seek the opinions of others in the group.
- Help the shyest person by drawing him/her into the conversation. Encourage the person by saying, "Let's hear your opinion on this" or simply, "What do you think?"
- Ask or introduce 'what if' questions. This is an excellent way to start a conversation in a group. It can also help to pep up the conversation if there is a lull. It is important that the 'what 'if' question is the one that appeals to and interests everyone in the group.
- Do not monopolise or dominate the conversation. Even a brilliant or gifted conversationalist gets on the nerves of people and bores them if he talks endlessly. So, do not go on and on. Do not over-converse. If you are narrating any event or story or joke, keep it short and sweet. Be brief.
- Do not grill your partner. You are not a CBI investigator. It is not necessary to find out the minutest details of other people's lives. Do not overstep your limits and subject the other person to a third degree.

If your party is small and all people know each other, then conversation becomes fairly easy. In such a setting, it is possible for you to direct the flow, choose subjects for discussion, take the conversation in the direction you want it to go or encourage the person you want to take part and get involved in what is going on. You will do all this to ensure that all your guests are having a good time. Again, take care to see that you only control and direct the setting and that you do not dominate the proceedings.

In today's society and culture, there is an increasing

permissiveness. Words which hitherto were never used in polite society are now being freely bandied about even in mixed groups. Topics which were considered too personal and too sensitive are being widely discussed. Talk shows and reality shows make up issues/subjects which were never talked about in the drawing room earlier. In this scenario, one may be tempted to introduce taboo subjects. Do not presume that everybody is comfortable with such subjects. Use discretion. It is best and safest to avoid such topics notwithstanding the prevalent permissive culture.

Chapter 16

A SENSE OF HUMOUR

J Mencius said, "The great man is he who does not lose his child's heart." And a child's heart is full of humour and laughter. William Fry, MD, Professor of Psychiatry, reports that on an average, a kindergarten student laughs 300 times a day. Yet, adults average only 19 laughs a day. Why the difference? Are we too uptight? Too tense? Do we take life too seriously? Isn't it time we learnt to relax?

We are more apt to display a sense of humour when we are ourselves, when we are natural. We become devoid of humour when we are pompous, pretentious, obviously hiding a feeling of insecurity. Humour is the balm for anyone who takes oneself too seriously, who is unable to let go of tension even for a moment. A sense of humour is a gift you can give yourself all year round. According to Henry Ward Beecher, "A man without a sense of humour is like a wagon without springs... he is jolted disagreeably by every little pebble on the road."

Our five senses are not enough for ideal living. We need to use our sixth sense-our sense of humour. Humour isn't about merely telling jokes' it is the way we view the world, the picture we take, the attitude we adopt: it is a way of life. We can be sincere about life without taking it too seriously (after all, you won't get out of it alive anyway!). We can laugh at our mistakes and stupidities, the frailties and foibles of human beings. Do take your work/job/profession seriously, but do not take yourself too seriously.

The Greek philosopher Plato remarked that "Even the Gods love humour and jokes." This must be correct, because the value of laughter is recorded in all sacred scriptures. To quote only one example, Muhammad, the Prophet of Islam, is reported to have said that "He deserves paradise who makes his companions laugh." J Menander said, "Whoever makes you laugh helps you to live." Abraham Lincoln, under tremendous pressure and tension during his presidency, stated "But for my sense of humour, I would have succumbed to the strains and pressures of office."

There are many benefits of humour and laughter. The benefits of humour are too numerous to ignore:

- Humour gives us a sense of hope. It enlivens us when we are down. It calms tempers and soothes jangled nerves. It is a safety valve which keeps us sane and relaxed.
- Having a sense of humour is one of the greatest assets of happy and successful people. When a number of managers were asked what they looked for and deemed to be a personal asset, 80% answered "a sense of humour". Likewise, in 'male partners wanted' ads, 80% of women stated that they would prefer a partner with a good sense of humour.
- When you make fun of yourself, you disempower those who would make fun of you and disarm possible confrontations.
- Laughter dissolves tension, stress, anxiety, irritation, anger, grief and depression because if you can laugh at it, you can live with it. A person without a sense of humour is like a car without shock absorbers.
- Medical research has come to the conclusion that laughter boosts the immune system.
- Laughter reduces pain by releasing endorphins that

are more potent than equal amount of morphine.

- Humour helps to integrate both hemispheres of our brain — the left deciphers the verbal content while the right interprets whether it is funny or not.
- Laughter adds spice to life; it is to life what salt is to a hard-boiled egg.
- Develop your sense of humour and you will find you are more productive, a better communicator and a superior team player.
- Everyone loves someone who can make them laugh. The more you share your sense of humour, the more friends you will have.
- Humour brings the balance we need to get through the turbulence of life comfortably.
- Laughter is even equivalent to a small amount of exercise. It massages all the organs of the body, according to Dr. James Walsh.
- A sense of humour can help you accept the inevitable, rise to any challenge, handle the unexpected with ease, and come out of any difficulty smiling.

In view of the above, it is no surprise that the great comedian Charlie Chaplin affirmed that "The most wasted day is that in which we have not laughed."

It is obvious that it is most desirable that one develops a sense of humour. We outline a few tips on how to develop your own unique sense of humour:

- Start by reading humorous books, jokes, watching funny movies, watching comedy television, looking at videos of comedy classics, joining humour clubs, exchanging jokes with family, friends, co-workers and also on the social media.
- When visiting someone in the hospital, take funny greeting cards and humorous books instead of or in addition to flowers.

- Look for and find humour in every situation around you.
- Surround yourself with fun-loving and positive people.
- Avoid negative self-talk, negative situations and negative people.
- Give yourself permission to have fun and to laugh. It is a good feeling to release the child or the clown within you.
- Become comfortable with the thought that it is ok to be silly. When things get too serious, nonsense sometimes makes the best sense.
- Collect humorous material and start your own humour library.
- When things are stressful, try to look for the humour in the situation. If you can think or say to yourself, "Someday, I am going to laugh about this", then don't wait! Laugh about it now!
- Schedule your own humour and relaxation breaks.

Finally, remember that a sense of humour is all about taking your job, your profession, your work, your commitments, your relationships, etc. seriously; but taking yourself tightly. Therefore, travel light. In the words of GK Chesterton, "Angels fly because they take themselves lightly." So can you!

Chapter 17

THE ART OF PRESENTATION

The importance of speaking well cannot be over-emphasized. Most of the time- we communicate through speaking because it is so natural and spontaneous. But speaking before an audience (public speaking) is an art that has to be learnt with great care and serious effort.

In industry and commerce, the term presentation has come to be used in preference to 'public speaking'. In a separate chapter, we have covered, in great detail, the subject of public speaking. The Art of Presentation has certain distinctive features and we shall touch upon these in this chapter.

Presentations: Occasions and Definition

As mentioned earlier, in business, the term 'presentation' is preferred to the term 'public speaking'. The reason, it appears, is that the purpose of a presentation is more precisely and concretely defined. There are many occasions when presentations are made, such as:

- Launch of a new product or service
- Making a marketing or sales proposal
- Diversification of business
- Presenting a new business plan

- Starting a training course/session
- Contribution to a conference or seminar

Speaking before an audience on any of the occasions mentioned, or on a similar one, is a serious matter. It requires careful preparation that cannot satisfactorily be done by one person alone. Therefore, a presentation has been defined as a formal or set-piece occasion with two usual hallmarks.

- The use of audio-visual aids
- Teamwork

Looked at in this way, a presentation stands out as a speech made with the help of at least one teammate on the basis of sufficient material/information gathered and processed for a significant business occasion and delivered with the help of audio-visual aids in order to make a positive impact on the audience.

Guidelines for making successful presentations

Be clear about the occasion

This means that the person proposing to make a presentation must know his proper sphere and the purpose he wants to fulfil through his presentation. The speaker should also be absolutely clear about the context in which the presentation is to be made.

Conduct audience analysis

It is of utmost importance to know and understand the audience for whom the presentation is meant. An audience is not just a gathering of individuals at one place. It has a collective personality of its own. The size of the audience, the age, sex, educational background, experience, nationality, etc. of the audience have great relevance to the presentation. For example, it is important to know whether one is going to make a presentation before an all-male, all-female or a mixed audience. It will influence the speaker's choice of words, tone, need for details, illustrations and so on. It will also give us an idea of their expectations and their likely reactions to what the speaker is going to say.

Moreover, audience analysis should continue during the presentation. The body language of the audience gives valuable and much needed feedback to the speaker. For this purpose, the speaker must keep his/her eyes and ears open. The audience's smiles, stares — whether blank or excited — silent whispers or lip movement will give the presenter an idea of their reactions and guide him/her through the presentation.

Visit/have an idea of the location

The speaker should not take the location for granted. He must make it a point to visit the location before the event. A lot depends on the size of the room, seating arrangements, room temperature, lighting controls, public address equipment, audio-visual equipment, acoustics, etc. If, for example, the room echoes or resounds with the words one speaks, much of the presentation will be spoilt. Or, if the audience is large and the public-address arrangements are not satisfactory, both the audience and presenter will get irritated.

Plan the presentation

The next, and perhaps the most important step is to plan the presentation in detail or at least in outline, showing exactly what you propose to say at the beginning, the middle and the end of the presentation. A rough plan may be as follows:

Decide upon the method of presentation

In practice, three methods of presentation have been observed:

Reading: Many speakers write out their entire speeches and read them out before the audience. The greatest advantage of this method is that accuracy is best maintained in it. But most of us do not read aloud well. Most readers sink into monotones, miss punctuation marks and fumble for words. They may also lose eye contact with the audience. So, this method has more disadvantages than advantages.

Memorised presentation: Some speakers write and memorise the entire speech. Their memory is powerful enough to remember everything, including the pauses. But very few have been able to use this method effectively. The greatest disadvantage of this method is that the speaker may forget some important point/part of the script. Trying to then locate it in the script, if it is with the speaker at the moment, spoils the entire effect of the presentation. That is why most of the speakers memorise key parts and use notes to help them during the presentation.

Extemporaneous presentation: This is the most popular method used by really effective speakers. They have carefully planned their speeches, but then they speak as if they were getting the ideas, coherently arranged, on the spur of the moment. Whenever they need any help they look into their notes that they keep handy. Looking into the notes, serially arranged, seems quite natural and the speech delivered in this manner also sounds spontaneous.

Rehearse the presentation

There are five important Ps of presentation. These are:

Planning | Preparation | Practice | Practice | More Practice

As a necessary part of the preparation, rehearsal is crucially important. It helps to gain confidence and work towards self-improvement. Rehearsing the speech is only one part of the preparation. The rehearsal also gives the speaker a clear idea of when, where and how to introduce/bring in visual aids to support the presentation. Only a rehearsal can ensure coordination of effort.

Consider personal aspects

The speaker himself/herself is essentially a part of the message. The audience first sees the speaker, then listens to the spoken words. Therefore, it is crucial that the speaker displays a presentable appearance. Since it is a formal occasion, the speaker must be formally dressed. If the speaker is well prepared and properly dressed for the occasion, he/she will not only look good, but also feel confident. And confidence is the primary characteristic of an effective presentation.

Confidence is clearly reflected in a clear, strong and well-modulated voice. It may require many hours of preparation and practice to acquire this. The speaker can also train himself in establishing effective and appealing eye contact, acquiring the correct posture and learning meaningful gestures. There is also an immense scope for improvement in facial expressions and manner of walking. The way one walks before one's audience at once conveys an impression — that of confidence, or the lack of it.

Using visual aids

A presentation is meant primarily to convey information. This is the first and foremost function of communication. And to make this function effectively, the communicator/speaker making the presentation often has to rely on visual aids such as whiteboards, pictures, charts, PowerPoint presentations, etc.

There is quite a large range of visual aids in use. There is no visual aid to suit all purposes.

Needless to say, any visual aid that is used must be easily visible to the audience. It should also be ensured that the speaker, while speaking and moving, does not obstruct the view of the aid. A suitable position, therefore, may be like in the figure shown below:

Guidelines for the use of visual aids

Visual aids are used to convey key parts of the message. They help to emphasis the most vital points of the presentation. No hard and fast rules can be laid down for the use of visual aids in all presentations. Much depends on the individual's choice. However, the following points may be of help to speakers in general:

- As already stated, make sure that everyone in the audience is able to see the visual aid clearly.
- The speaker must explain the visual aid and state clearly if there is any likelihood that the audience may not immediately understand it.
- The visual aids must fit well into the presentation. They must be an essential part of the plan of the presentation.
- Proper emphasis must be laid on the visual aid. The speaker must point to it with bodily action and words.
- Sometimes, a long stick or a laser pointer must be used to draw the audience's attention to a certain portion of the visual aid.
- The speaker must largely look at the audience while speaking, not at the aid.
- If the speaker is using slides/transparencies, he must make sure that they are clearly numbered in the correct sequence and are kept the right way up. Any confusion in their order of arrangement will damage the presenter's image.
- No visual aid should be kept on for too long.
- The speaker should use pictures, drawings and colours for interest. One must remember: 'A picture says a thousand words'.
- A slide should carry only essential information.

- The content of the information on the slide should be kept limited to about 25 words or the equivalent in figures.

Chapter 18

PUBLIC SPEAKING

We live in a world where the ability to communicate is becoming increasingly important. One of the most effective ways of communicating, whether to motivate, to inform or simply to entertain, is public speaking.

Many people have opportunities to communicate in this manner. Yet, they hesitate because of inexperience or more likely, because of nerves. This is a pity, because nerves can be contained; stage fright can be overcome with the right approach and by making adequate effort. And with the right approach and effort, it is possible for almost anyone to make a competent speech.

The power of speech is an effective tool for personal success. By acquiring this ability, you can gain leadership, recognition, success and a winning personality. The ability to stand up in front of a group of people and persuade them to accept your ideas will give you a sense of tremendous strength and power. Speaking effectively before a group is a thrilling and exhilarating experience. Also, it can bring great success in your life. The magic of effective speech is an essential ingredient of leadership and success. Leadership naturally gravitates to the person who speaks well. A person who can speak well is credited with far more success than she/he sometimes actually deserves.

What is public speaking?

Simply put, it means speaking in public. One of the many definitions is "Public speaking is the art and science of establishing effective oral communication with an audience."

Communication is the art of being understood, the process of creating understanding and trust. To be effective, communication must evoke adequate understanding, an appropriate response and produce the desired result.

Audience means a group of targeted listeners. Two or more people who do not have any kind of very personal relationship with the speaker may form this group. Thus, speaking with friends, relatives or persons sharing special relationships do not constitute an audience.

Public speaking is not at all difficult. When learnt and practiced systematically, anyone can deliver a good speech. Effective public speaking is a tremendous confidence builder and booster. It not only helps you when speaking to a large audience, but also helps you to confidently and effectively handle your day to day activities such as business talks, sales pitches, presentations before clients, meetings with seniors, handling juniors, customer relations, friendly and social conversations, etc.

Nervousness and stage fright

All great speeches are characterised by nervousness. It is fairly natural. All good speakers, performers and actors are more prone to nervousness and stage fright than ordinary human beings. Nervousness is not bad. It shows your sensitivity, your seriousness and your intense desire to perform well. It is nervous energy. It can be converted to your benefit by proper control and direction. Channelize your nervous energy and convert it into strength, an asset. It will help you excel. Nervousness is bad only if it cripples you, paralyses you and inhibits you from coming forward to speak.

To overcome nervousness, one has to develop confidence through knowledge, practice and experience.

The greatest strength of a public speaker is that, by and large, his audience wants him/her to succeed. Capitalise on this. Be friendly towards your audience. Think of them as your friends. Speak to the friendly faces in the audience that you can easily spot. This will help you reduce your tension and ease your nervousness.

One reason for nervousness is that a beginner is very self-conscious. He is more conscious of himself than of the subject of his talk, the audience or the surroundings. So, to overcome stage fright, it is helpful to take the focus off yourself.

Also, welcome every opportunity to speak before a group. In fact, create such opportunities for yourself.

A few practical tips to overcome stage fright

There are three stages involved in this process:

Stage 1: Well in advance

- Do, on a regular basis, whatever it is that relaxes you — yoga, meditation, progressive relaxation techniques, etc.
- Prepare well — adequate preparation is the best antidote to nervousness.
- Think rationally. Do not catastrophise events. See things from a proper perspective.
- Practice affirmation and creative visualisation.

Stage 2: At the last minute

- Breathe deeply.
- Do isometric exercises while awaiting your turn.
- Try progressive relaxation exercises.

- Pray, if you are so inclined.
- Underplay the importance of the audience. Think of them as if they owe you money, or imagine they are vegetables, or visualize them looking very funny, etc. In short, do anything that will remove the awe and fear of the audience in your mind.
- Psyche yourself up, hold positive images. Remember past successes and give yourself a pep talk.
- Concentrate on your speech, instead of on yourself. Listen to other speeches. If possible, engage in friendly conversations with people around.

Stage 3: During the presentation

- Remember, you feel worse than you look. The audience does not know that you are nervous. Only you know it. Therefore, look confident. Fake it till you make it. Smile. You are a powerhouse generator. Establish a connection with the audience and your power will flow through and from you. You have great stuff in you and it will come out easily, naturally.
- Speak to the interested listeners.
- Concentrate on the here and now.

Platform presence of the public speaker

Every public speaker should:

- Be energetic and lively.
- Be enthusiastic about the speech, the subject, the occasion, the audience and of course, yourself.
- Be appropriately dressed: Good grooming is very important. The audience starts judging you even before you start speaking. First impressions are important and lasting. The first impression the audience will

have of you is that you are respectable, decent and nice. Therefore, have a pleasant, clean look. Smell good. When you look good, you feel good and when you feel good, you act good. Good grooming builds up your self-confidence.

- Elicit confidence: Be relaxed and at ease. Look happy.
- Be poised: Be calm, have equanimity and poise.
- Be pleasant and positive: Have a pleasant outlook, smile, genuinely and sincerely.
- Be friendly: Look at audiences as friends — talk in a friendly, conversational manner.
- Be natural: Do not imitate others. You are a unique person. Your personality is yours, develop and cultivate it. Do whatever naturally makes you a good speaker.
- Posture: Stand with both feet on the ground, feet slightly apart (neither too close nor too far), weight evenly balanced. Balance yourself on both feet without leaning or slouching. Stand fairly erect and comfortably upright, professionally relaxed. Do not sway. You do not have to be in military attention pose. Here's what not to do:
    - o Do not keep hands in pockets.
    - o Do not have your hands held behind you.
    - o Avoid crossing your arms.
    - o Avoid the fig-leaf position (covering your pelvic area with your palm)
- Gestures: Gestures are a natural accompaniment of speech. Without gestures, a speaker may appear dull. Gestures should be natural, dynamic and spontaneous. They should be free, open and full. Do not make half-gestures. Also, avoid wild gestures. Gestures should be varied, appropriate, uninhibited and well-timed.

Avoid too many gestures. Gestures are closely related to the speaker's personality. Therefore, gesture in front of an audience exactly as you would if you were having a lively, animated conversation with a friend — no more, no less.

Note: Avoid nervous gestures like ear-tugging, arm scratching, nose-picking, fiddling, etc. Avoid clapping when you come back to terminus (base position). These are signs of nervousness.

- Movement: Move deliberately to change mood or pace. Draw attention to visual aids or away from them, using movement. Reinforce ideas by stepping to a side or by leaning forward. Keep your shoulder orientation towards the audience. This is particularly relevant when you are using visual aids. Do not speak unless you have eye contact with the audience.
- Facial expression: Maintain relaxed, animated, conversational expressions. Do not have a stony, deadpan look.
- Eye contact: Maintaining eye contact is very important. It helps to establish rapport with the audience. It is a bridge between the speaker and the audience. It helps to hold the attention of the audience and the full personality of the speaker comes into play. It is also a source of immediate feedback to the speaker — it helps to pick up clues about audience's comprehension and opinions. Maintain eye contact with those persons who are sympathetic, keen and interested. Always look at:
    - o The entire group, not one section of it
    - o Good listeners who nod
    - o Key decision makers

Rule of thumb: Do not stare; move away eye contact from a person after 1-3 seconds. You may come back to them later. If you are at the beginning of your public speaking career, avoid looking at people in the audience:

- o Who are expressionless
- o Who are wide-eyed
- o Who wink/ blink
- o Who look bored or yawn

These people may adversely affect your confidence.

- Voice: Use your voice effectively. Speak with enthusiasm and energy. Do not speak monotonously. Modulate your voice and speak expressively. Speak in a warm, pleasant tone, not a distracting one (too high, nasal or whiny). Your voice quality is important. Do exercises — breathing exercises, tongue exercises, lip exercises, articulation exercises, etc. — to improve the quality of your voice.
- Volume: Speak audibly. Be appropriately loud; not too loud, not too soft.
- Speed: Speak at the correct speed and vary it. Go fast over less important parts of your speech and slow down while making important points.
- Pause: Pause effectively before and after making an important point. Pause before making a major break in thought. Pause before and after asking a question, telling a joke, story, quotation, etc. for more effect.
- Enunciation: Enunciate clearly and pronounce words well. Do not mumble. Avoid filler words such as 'you know', `ok', 'I mean', 'right', etc.

Other hints

- Do not speak when you are tired. Do not eat a lot before you speak.

- Try to bring your audience closer to one another. Do not let them sit in a scattered manner. A well-knit audience helps the speaker.
- Be time-conscious and brief. A short, well-prepared speech is always appreciated.
- Make yourself comfortable. Create space for yourself by moving chairs, etc. if necessary. Adjust to the environment and take your time. Do not rush into your speech. Indulge in some physical activity. Hold the audience's attention, smile and then speak.
- After completing your speech, do not rush back as soon as your speech is over. Wait for applause. And if it comes, accept it graciously. You deserve it.

Speech preparation

It is not advisable to speak without preparation. Have at least one basic, central thought around which you will prepare your speech.

Before starting to prepare your speech, ask yourself, why are you giving this talk? Who is your audience? What is the purpose of this talk in terms of the audience's interest? Answers to these questions will help you to design your talk and will make your objective (purpose of your talk) clear to you. Is it to entertain? To inform? To motivate? To sell? To persuade?

Speech outlines

There are some time-tested patterns for speech outlines:

- Introduction — body — conclusion
- Ho-hum (attract favourable attention)
  Why bring that up (arouse interest)
  For instance (give examples, instances, illustrations,

etc.)

So what? (appeal for action)

This four-point formula is called Borden's formula.

- Show what is wrong

  Show how to remedy it

  Appeal for action

- Why something has happened — cause

  What the results were — effects

  Show how required change can be brought about — remedy

- Attract favourable attention - present the problem

  Show and explain the problem

  Present all possible solutions with good/bad points

  Appeal for action

- Attract favourable attention

  Arouse interest in your proposition

  Convince audience of merits of your proposition

  Re-emphasize and summarise

  Appeal for action

Preparing a speech

- Start preparing immediately once you accept a speaking assignment. The earlier you begin, the better. Delay may cause tension and may lead to poor performance.
- Decide on the topic and choose the general coverage. Brood over, think and keep referring to various source materials. As you continue to think and brood various thoughts, ideas, facts, experiences, illustrations, information, arguments, stories, examples, quotations, etc. to support your speech objectives will come to

you at different times. Jot them down immediately. Capture them on paper as soon as possible. Delay will make you forget them.

- Arrange all your thoughts in the sequence of introduction-body-conclusion and write your speech fully. Edit this material for clarity, effectiveness and of course, time-limit. Do not cross the time limit. Stay within the time allocated to you. Bear in mind that the average speed of speaking is 120 words per minute.
- While preparing your speech, remember the purpose of your speech (to motivate, to inspire, to convince, to educate, to entertain, to inform, to show courtesy, to pay tribute, to build goodwill, etc.). Also, find out the type of audience and occasion. This will help you in the final preparation of your speech.
- Your speech may require editing and correcting a number of times. While doing so, remember that your speech is something that you are going to deliver as a talk. Therefore, keep the language and style conversational — as you use in a talk and not as in a written composition. Stories, examples, illustrations, etc. make a talk interesting, impressive, convincing and easy to remember. Humour adds spice. All the supporting materials must be vivid, impressive and related to your speech.
- Always include in the body of your speech, anecdotes, personal experiences, examples, comparisons, statistics, case histories, definitions, quotations, opinions, etc. Please remember that all these aids which you use must support your subject and should be relevant to it.
- Practice your speech many times. This will instil confidence. Record your speech and play it back. This will provide you valuable feedback.

- Lastly, remember that a well-prepared speech is already 9/10th delivered. Do not sit down and try to manufacture a speech in 30 minutes. A speech must grow from within.

Supporting materials (to make a speech more effective)

- Graphic oriented comparisons: These can be used to point out similarities between that which is already known or believed and that which is not (for example, God and electricity).
- Specific illustration: This helps to paint pictures. The audience thinks in pictures. It is most effective and creates immediate rapport with the audience. Here is an example: A young boy was sitting near a lake. He observed some fish swimming. He was very fond of eating fish. So, he exclaimed, "I wish I could have fish for dinner!" The local priest happened to pass by and heard the boy's words. He gently tapped the boy's shoulders and said, "Young man, if you want to have fish for dinner, stop wishing and start fishing."
- Specific instances: If the speaker gives a relevant personal example, it will lend immense credibility and authenticity to the speech.
- Statistics: When properly used, statistics are very effective. Otherwise, they put the audience to sleep. Statistics should not be too many. Also, they should be specific/graphic and not general. A good specific statistic is effective in establishing a point, clinching an argument, etc.
- Unprejudiced material: Quotations and testimonials of well-qualified persons who are experts in the field lend enormous support and credibility.

- Restatement of ideas: This leads to remembrance and the best speech is the one that is remembered the longest. Please ensure that you restate ideas and not repeat them.
- Visual aids: What we see impacts us more than what we hear. A good picture is worth a thousand words. Use visual aids appropriately. Visual aids are meant to support/supplement the speaker and not supplant him. The speaker is his/her own best visual aid. The subtle variations of expressions played on his face and parts of his body, his voice modulation, gestures, etc. contribute in a large measure to the effectiveness of the speech or the lack of it.

Opening and closing of a speech

A good speech is like a good flight: easy take off, smooth landing, cruise in between and keep the distance between the two as short as possible.

Every talk needs a good opening and closing.

Opening of a speech

- Do not be apologetic: For example, do not start with: “I don’t think I can do justice to this topic” or “This is a dry subject.”
- Do not weep: For example, do not start with “I have a sore throat” or “I have not prepared my speech.”
- Arouse curiosity: Add a little suspense right at the beginning.
- Relate a human-interest story: Who does not like a story?
- Ask a question: A question designed to impel the audience to think out the matter, has already started

the attention process. After the question, pause for a very short moment.

- Relate to the audience's vital interests.
- Start with shocking facts.
- Open with a striking quotation.
- Show an exhibit.
- Start with a short, related story, preferably in a dialogue form. Humanise it.
- Compliment the audience.
- Link yourself with the audience: Use statements such as "I am one of you", "I love Mumbai too", etc.
- Talk something of momentary interest: For example, refer to the chairman's statement, a previous speaker's remark, or something in the room.
- Use humour cleverly: This method is a little dicey. It may misfire, and the audience may not respond to your joke the way you wanted them to do. Resort to this method only if you are certain that you can tell a joke well and effectively. If you can make the audience laugh at the beginning, you have won. But if your joke falls flat, your confidence is likely to be shattered, especially if you are a beginner. Therefore, use a joke at the beginning only if you can handle it well. And remember, a joke is only the icing on the cake and not the cake itself. A joke should be relevant, not vulgar, have no double-meaning and should not be against a religion/community.

Closing the speech

The closing is very important because what is said last is likely to be remembered the most. Build a climax and stop. Stop, do not merely talk of stopping.

Resist the temptation to continue talking after the climax. Do not let the applause of the audience lure you to talk further. You should stop at a time when the audience still wants you to continue talking. The audience should feel sad that you have stopped and not glad that you have stopped. They should feel: "I wish he'd talk more!" and not: "Why does he not stop?!"

Sometimes, somewhere during your speech, you may reach a natural climax. It is better to stop here because it needs great skills and acumen to steer the speech further with equal interest. Please remember the essential point is the impact of your speech- the end result —and not complete delivery of whatever you have prepared. The sooner you achieve this result, the better the speaker that you are.

The closing of the speech is an integral and essential part of the speech. Therefore, it should be planned in advance. Round off your talk effectively. It is the grand finale.

Never end your speech with words like "This is all I have to say, so I will stop now." This is a very weak closing.

Some examples: If it is a social occasion, you can conclude your speech with a joke. If it is a business meeting, it could be statistical or a solution to a specific problem. If it is a public meeting to discuss special civil matters, the conclusion should be a definite demand for action.

Time-tested ways of effective closing

- Summarise your main ideas.
- Appeal for action. For example, "Let us donate", "Let us boycott", "Let us vote", etc.
- End with an appropriate quotation: A fitting, meaningful quotation at the end will bring about a meaningful and happy conclusion in almost all cases.
- Close in a humorous vein. Tell a fitting joke and leave them laughing.
- End on a poetic note with an appropriate verse.

- Close with an illustrative story that conveys the essence of what you have been telling them in your speech — and stop.
- Finally, remember to 'be gone'. Do not hold on to the dais. A good speaker should be brief, cheerful and gone!

How to make your speech more effective

- Know the audience
- Avoid big words; use simple language.
- Avoid weasel (waffle) words such as "Many such things like that", "all sorts of things", "something like that", "so on and so forth", "ok", "I mean", etc.
- Use comparisons and contrasts: For example, "Sunshine and darkness, gaiety and sorrow is the inexorable law of life" or "A man without ambition is like a body without a soul."
- Give examples and illustrations. The more, the better.
- Use 'we' and not I. As a speaker, it helps to show that the speaker is one of the audience - the audience will love you for it.
- Tune in to the listeners' wave-length.
- Give the audience what it likes and not what you like. As they say, to a baker, give bread; to a butcher, give mutton; when both are present, give mutton sandwich.
- Adopt the KISS formula: Keep It Short and Simple.
- Adopt the AIDS formula: Attract Attention, arouse Interest, create Desire and stimulate Action.
- Do not memories the entire speech, only the main points.
- Use the right verbs, adverbs and adjectives. They give power and punch to the language. Here are two

important rules:

- When there is a choice between a noun and a verb form, always prefer a verb. For example, instead of saying "My father gave me advice to..." say, "My father advised me to..."
- When there is a choice between an adjective and a verb form, again, prefer the verb. For example, instead of saying "You can develop a rich vocabulary by..." say, "You can enrich your vocabulary by..."
- Use effective pauses.
- As a good speaker, be brief, precise, clear, speak with conviction, follow a logical sequence and be specific, not abstract.

Adding humour to your speech

- The purpose of humour is to entertain the audience and sometimes, provide relief.
- Jokes should be relevant and appropriate to the subject at hand.
- Jokes should never be vulgar or offensive. Never joke on a religion or community.
- Cut a joke on yourself, victimize yourself. The audience will love you for that.
- When you like a joke, share it with at least ten different people. This practice will help you remember the joke at the appropriate times.

Audience analysis

Before speaking, try to determine the following general facts about the audience:

- Number of people expected

- Age group of the audience
- Sex ratio of the audience (gender balance)
- Their occupational relationship with the speaker or the organization to which they are connected (such as customers, colleagues, senior managers, etc.)
- Educational level and background of the audience
- Open-mindedness of the audience — are they willing to accept the ideas that you may present?
- Their knowledge of the subject at hand.
- Their reasons for attending (seeking information, forced to attend, etc.)
- Their opinion towards the subject (favourable, hostile, etc.)
- Their attitude towards the speaker
- Their attitude towards the conclusion
- Benefits of listening to the speaker, for the audience
- Disadvantages of listening to the speaker, for the audience

Answers to these questions will help you design and frame your speech appropriately.

Suggestions for giving a good speech of introduction

A speech of introduction is like a social introduction — your job is to bring the speaker & audience together.

Thoroughly prepare the speech of introduction. It should not be for more than 2-3 minutes.

- Collect the speaker's bio-data in advance.
- Collect the details of the topic and the title of the speech in advance.
- Be certain of the name of the speaker and its correct

pronunciation.

- Be sincere and straightforward in your introduction. Avoid undue flattery and flowery language.
- If the bio-data is very long, highlight the points that are relevant to the talk, topic and occasion and will be of interest to the audience.

When you get up to speak:

- Address the Chair and the House (do not include the name of the speaker in the salutation).
- Give the exact title of the speaker's subject and show how and why it is of special interest to the audience.
- Give the bio-data in brief. While quoting the qualifications and other details, refer to those that relate to the topic of the speech.
- Say the speaker's name clearly and distinctly.
- Be enthusiastic in your introduction. Pause a while before giving his name. Pause between the first and the last name and say it with force and vigour.
- While giving his name, do not turn to him but look at the audience. After stating the full name, turn to the speaker. Raise your voice while stating the name of the speaker.
- Never discuss the subject. Never suggest that the speaker will talk about a certain aspect of the subject.
- Use language in the third person. For example, "Mr. Kapil Mehra will talk to us..." instead of "You will talk to us..."
- Sell the topic and the speaker in the shortest time possible. Adopt the TIS (topic, interest, speaker) formula. State the topic, talk of how it is of interest to the audience and then state why the speaker is the best qualified person to talk about it.

Proposing a vote of thanks

- Address the Chair and the audience. In salutation, do not include the name of the speaker for whom you are proposing the vote of thanks.
- Thank the speaker for having graced the occasion and for sparing valuable time to be with the audience.
- Make a reference to the speech. You may mention about the wit and wisdom of the speaker and the intelligent way in which the subject was handled.
- Propose a vote of thanks... "And now ladies and gentlemen, I propose a hearty vote of thanks to Ms. ABC and I am confident you will carry it with a loud applause."
- Keep your speech as short as possible. Do not summarise the speaker's speech or give your views on the subject. Never criticise the speech or evaluate it. The purpose of the vote of thanks is to make the speaker feel happy.
- Thank all those who have contributed to the success of the event — organisers, sponsors, media, sound system managers, caterers, etc. and of course, the audience.

Microphone techniques

- Use a mic at every given opportunity. It is the most powerful aid for a public speaker. It helps to address large audiences with little effort. But it does not turn a bad speaker into a good speaker. It merely amplifies the voice of a speaker. Before starting, make sure that the mic is switched on. Do not start speaking without testing it. If you do, it may embarrass you, disturb the audience and create some innocent laughter. No speaker can afford this diversion. It creates a poor impression.

- To test the mic, tap it with the index finger or the back of its second knuckle. The sound of the tap should reverberate, and the speaker should be able to hear its echo.
- Adjust the mic. Take your time to adjust the height, fitting, position, etc. even if it means keeping the people waiting. Do not hurry out of panic or nervousness. Keep the head of the mic at least six inches away from your lips. Also adjust for volume. If you are using a hand mic, make sure you maintain the appropriate distance between the lips and the mic at all times.
- While speaking, stay at least six inches away from the mic. Do not come too close to it or go too far. Make sure you test the audibility of your voice.
- If the mic stops functioning in the middle of your speech, do not panic. Stop confidently. Request for having it adjusted. Take your time. If audibility is restored, and if the general atmosphere permits it, make a joke about this mechanical marvel.
- If the mic cannot be adjusted or remedied, speak without it. Remember what Winston Churchill said, "Now that science has failed, let's get back to nature." If the size of the hall and the audience makes it impossible for you to speak without the mic, then do not speak at all as it will only unnecessarily strain you and the audience.
- If you are directing remarks to the left of the room looking in that direction, then move to the right of the mic, so that everybody will be able to hear you; and vice versa.
- Do not speak too fast and not too loud.

Chapter 19

RESUME BUILDING

A resume (also sometimes referred to as a bio-data or curriculum vitae [CV], though different from those), is the single most important document in the entire interview and selection process. It is the first step in the selection process. It is your introduction to the interviewer and explains your complete background — education, experience, achievements and character. It reflects your personality and is seen even before you are called for an interview. It is your photograph, your passport, your salesman, your Ambassador.

Writing a resume helps you assess your pluses and minuses. A good resume will not, by itself, get you a job, but a poor one will surely kill all chances of getting one. Notwithstanding this, many candidates give cursory attention to this document and many resumes are rejected on the basis of the manner in which they are presented. A typical bad resume suffers from the following undesirable features:

- It is written or printed on crumpled or stained paper.
- It contains numerous spelling mistakes.
- Proper communication mechanisms (phone number, email, etc.) are missing.
- Incomplete or wrong information is given.
- There are typographical errors.

Since the resume is a key document, it should be presented very elegantly, neatly and attractively. It should be electronically typed on white, executive bond, A4-sized paper. It should not contain any spelling or typing mistakes. It should be submitted along with a covering letter that should also be electronically typed and printed on white, A4-sized executive bond paper, which should be clean and not creased. Maintain proper spacing and margins.

In short, to win the first round in the selection process, it is crucial to take great care of preparing the resume.

The resume, combined with a covering letter, demonstrates your writing skills, your ability to express ideas concisely, your eye for details and most importantly, your career focus. The resume should help to sum up the candidate's profile and should not contain too many details. Avoid irrelevant data. At the same time, it should not be inadequate. In other words, it should be neither too lengthy nor too short. A good resume should catch the prospective employer's attention.

Although resumes are vitally important documents, they are seldom read. The recruiters are sometimes too busy to read resumes that they receive in hundreds. They merely rapidly scan the resume for basic qualifications and work experience highlights. Your prospective employer looks for the critical qualifications. Therefore, endeavour to make your resume stand out. Always send the resume with the covering letter in a large envelope, so you do not have to fold it. It will stand out compared to those sent folded.

Quantify achievements

To be more effective and impactful, mention achievements and accomplishments instead of merely listing out activities. For example, "I play football" is an activity. An achievement could be "I captained the Mumbai University football team which won the inter-university tournament." Similarly, "I sing" is an activity. "I won the first prize in the inter-collegiate singing competition" is an achievement. Relating to work situations, mention targets met, new systems or procedures introduced by you, etc.

Do not make false claims about your achievements. Never fudge your resume.

It is important to state your career objective clearly. End the resume with a list of references (at least three). They should be people who are associated with you and your work, such as Principals of colleges, professors, managers, persons of social standing who know you well. Close relatives do not make credible references.

To make sure all goes well, list references with correct spellings of name, designation, address and proper phone number. References are important because every organization likes to ensure that when they recruit you, they are selecting a law-abiding, honest and reliable person. It is both difficult and time-consuming for the organization to independently verify your antecedents.

References of responsible persons who can vouch for you, fulfil this need. The higher the status of your referee, the higher would be your credibility.

Before using his name, write to the referee first, seeking permission to use his/her name in the resume. It will help to send a copy of the resume to the referee. Good organizations will contact your referees to authenticate your character. If you are sending your resume to many firms, then change references because if they are called too often, the referees may become less enthusiastic and indifferent.

In addition to the foregoing, please ensure that:

- You quote the reference code (mentioned in the job advertisement) correctly.
- You superscribe the envelope, if the advertisement mentions this requirement.
- You do not write anything in the space mentioned "For office use only" in an application form.

- If a particular format is advised, use only that format.
- Mention correct phone numbers and addresses.
- Avoid spelling mistakes, wrong name of the company, newspaper, etc.
- Enclose appropriate copies of certificates or other documents as needed.

A simple, effective resume will have the following components:

- Name: Write your name in the following order: First name — middle name — last name
- Date of birth: This must be in the date — month — year format, with the month ideally mentioned in words, such as 23 October, 1976.
- Address. Give an address where somebody can receive the correspondence. It is both frustrating and amusing for selectors to receive applications without forwarding addresses. Such applications inevitably find their way to the waste paper basket.
- Academic qualifications: The academic career must be listed with the most recent qualifications first, i.e. in the reverse chronological order.
- Professional/technical qualifications: These should also be in the reverse chronological order.
- Languages known: This information may be categorized under three heads: can speak, can read, can write.
- Work experience: Like academic qualifications, this must also be in the reverse chronological order. Remember to emphasize the achievements, not the regular work activities.
- Extra-curricular activities: Make sure that you have adequate knowledge of the activities you are listing, because the interviewer might quiz you on this. As

mentioned earlier, list achievements rather than activities.

- References: This has been explained earlier.
- Photograph: A passport-sized photograph enhances the quality of the resume. Get your picture clicked when you are fresh, clean, bright and looking your best. Although it is not mandatory to attach a photograph unless asked for in the advertisement, it is a good idea to send it in any case.
- Signature: The cover letter must be signed, but the resume need not be: This is an acknowledgement that the information given in the document is authentic and that you stand by it.
- But it is desirable that the resume is signed.

Chapter 20

GROUP DISCUSSION

Group Discussion (GD) is a very powerful screening device to judge the right candidates for educational courses, jobs, scholarships, etc. It is a part of, or a step in the entire selection process. GD is resorted to for the following two reasons:

To save time — by means of a GD, the selection panel can judge several candidates simultaneously

One's behaviour in a group is a vital part of one's total personality. GD enables the selectors to observe candidates in a group. Every organization ultimately is a collection of people who work together to achieve a common goal. Therefore, to be able to work effectively in a group is the fundamental reality of an organizational life. This ability increases the general all-round efficiency.

In a GD, the following are measured:

Content

This is evaluated by the grip the candidate has on the topic, depth of knowledge, the originality of views and the ability to present points of view clearly, systematically and logically.

Communication Skills

i. This is displayed by the candidate's ability to present

one's ideas logically and forcefully in an appropriately loud and well-modulated voice, together with the right rate of speech and good command over language, correct choice of words, correct pronunciation and enunciation, accompanied by smile, eye contact, gesture, adequate pauses, etc. All this will help to enhance the quality of one's communication.

ii. Communication skills include the art of listening—a very important but often neglected aspect of communication. Listening includes the ability to accept and integrate the views/opinions of others with one's own.

Psychological and emotional maturity

In a GD, the atmosphere can become highly charged. Tension and pressure may build up as candidates vie against each other to get selected. This situation may lead to a lack of consideration of and insensitivity to the feelings of the other members of the group. In these circumstances, some members become excited, emotionally aroused, loud, argumentative and over-bearing while others may become very quiet and withdraw from the discussion. Neither of these two attitudes or responses is desirable. The candidate that the selectors seek and choose is a person who is calm, cool, unruffled, balanced, in control of oneself and is, at the same time, assertively and effectively participating in the discussion.

Leadership qualities

The assessors also look for leadership qualities of the candidates. There is a general misconception that the person who speaks first, becomes the leader of the group. This is not true. Leadership gravitates to the person who displays his/her worth through the quality, originality and the content of his/her contribution. The leader also listens well and encourages silent, shy members to offer their views. The leader also diffuses the situation in case of heated arguments.

Thus, there are three specific skills which must be cultivated if a candidate wishes to enhance one's effectiveness in a GD:

Personal skills

The successful candidate will be the one who is relaxed, pleasant, courteous, co-operative (not cold and aloof), self-confident, assertive (not aggressive) and displays initiative. He/she also must have a good grasp of the subject, deep knowledge, the ability to think consistently, organise thoughts logically and coherently and present facts adequately.

Group skills

Group skills would include:

- Ability to communicate ideas fluently and effectively.
- Ability to listen.
- Willingness to listen to reason and logic.
- Ability to relate to others in the group.
- Ability to take sustain interest in the proceedings.
- Ability to see the topic from different angles and to encourage or steer the group to discuss the topic from different dimensions.
- Ability to generally enhance the quality of the discussion, to add value to the group and to build on valid points made by others.

Leadership skills

These include, inter alia, the following:

- Ability to take initiative.
- Ability to draw silent members into the discussion.
- Ability to persuade, convince, influence and carry the others with self.
- Ability to coordinate and summarise.
- Ability to diffuse the situation if necessary.
- Ability to control or tactfully keep in check the person who talks too much and tries to dominate the discussion.
- Ability to deal tactfully with irrelevant contributions.

In light of the foregoing, we can draw up a list of do's and don'ts which will enable you to perform better in a GD.

Do's for effective participation in a GD

- Display initiative
- Display a high level of content/quality
- Display confidence
- Display team spirit
- Display ability to diffuse a situation
- Communicate ideas fluently and effectively
- Listen attentively
- Maintain eye contact with members of the group
- Smile—give pleasant vibes, show warmth
- Be pleasant, courteous, affable, relaxed
- Be natural — do not adopt an alien accent or style
- Be assertive
- Be open (to new ideas)
- Encourage all members to participate
- Pay attention to posture, tone of voice, dress

- Adhere to all instructions — however minor
- Keep the discussions on the subject or bring it back to the subject if it has strayed away
- Deal tactfully with irrelevant contributions from others
- Try to control the persons who talk too much — see that no one monopolises the discussion
- Focus all your efforts and energy on consistently making points that will enhance the quality of the discussion
- Develop the ability to make original points that steer the group into discussing different angles/dimensions of the topic

Don'ts in a GD

- Don't brag or boast
- Don't go on an 'I' trip
- Don't be supercilious
- Don't be argumentative
- Don't pull others down
- Don't hurt, insult or humiliate others
- Don't attack others on religious, personal, regional or linguistic grounds
- Don't dominate the discussion
- Don't be aggressive
- Don't use foul language
- Don't use slang.
- Don't interrupt others
- Don't shout down a group member while trying to win over a viewpoint
- Don't use abbreviations and acronyms

- Don't harp on small points, thereby obscuring the critical issues
- Avoid personal arguments
- Avoid sub-grouping tendencies— persons who lack self-confidence generally tend to converse with other members instead of talking to the entire group directly.

Chapter 21

JOB INTERVIEW

An interview may be defined as a face to face meeting for the purpose of obtaining a statement or for assessing the qualities and suitability of a candidate. 'Interview' is derived from the French word 'entrevoir' which means 'glimpse'. Thus, there are two possible objectives of an interview:

- To obtain a statement or opinion of say, for example, a leading sports person or a film star or a statesman/ high-level politician or even the Prime Minister/ President of a country.
- To assess a person for selection, such as, for example, interviews for jobs, for promotions, for admissions to school/college or even a matrimonial alliance.

We will restrict our discussion to job interviews. A job interview may be defined as a meeting (online or offline) between two persons or a group of persons for assessing the suitability of a candidate. While the primary purpose is to determine whether the candidate will be good for the vacant role, a good interview is where the suitability of both the parties for each other is assessed/discussed.

An organization has a stake in the interview because human resources are its most valuable assets. It, therefore, is interested in recruiting the right person for the right job. In other words, just as a candidate is looking for a good job in a good organization, the organization also looks for good people.

This information, if internalized, helps you reduce your fear and awe as a candidate and helps you prepare better for an interview.

An interview process for the candidate can be broken into the following steps:

Pre-interview preparation

One of the most fundamental factors that contribute to the success of an interview is the time and quality of preparation made by the candidate. This will help to reduce uncertainty and anxiety prior to the interview. The amount of effort a candidate puts into the preparation will depend on the importance of the interview for him/her. If it is more important, he/she will put in more efforts to face the interview.

In the pre-interview stage, the candidate is advised to do the following:

- Keep oneself well-informed about current events, important national and international problems, issues and topics of general interest.
- Learn about the organization. It is important to know the background of the company in which you are seeking a job. A candidate should make himself aware of:
    - A brief history of the organization
    - Its main line of activity
    - Its expansion plans
    - Nature of products and services
    - Location of its various plants/offices/units/ divisions
- All this information can be gleaned from the following sources:
    - The company's website
    - The company's balance sheets

- o The chairperson's speech at the Annual General Body Meeting
- o Brochures and other marketing literature of the company

Making the effort to collect all this information will impress the interviewers about your keenness, enthusiasm and initiative.

- Know the job content. Find out the nature of the job and what you are expected to perform.
- If you are already employed, then know a lot about your present job and company.
- A reasonable revision of the subjects studied at college is desirable as interviewers often ask questions on the candidate's academic specialization. An interviewer judges your ability to grasp and retain what you will be taught by the organization in the future, on the basis of how you did it in the past with your past education and experience. The interviewer also evaluates your intelligence through this.
- List your positives and match oneself with the requirements of the job. What is required, how will you fit in, how will you make up for deficiencies or short-comings, if any, are important questions to be prepared for.
- Visit the site/place before the interview. This will help to ensure punctuality on the day of the interview. It will also help you to get a feel of the organization and reduce stress.
- Take care to have all relevant certificates, documents, testimonials handy. Every claim of achievement must ideally be supported by an appropriate document.
- Decide about your grooming and take appropriate action, if needed, such as a haircut, getting the right clothes, etc.

The day of the interview

- Ensure that you reach on time. Respect the interviewer's time by coming 10-15 minutes before the scheduled time. This will help you to settle down and familiarize yourself with the surroundings and release nervousness. If you go late for an interview, you may be summarily rejected because it reflects unprofessionalism.
- An interview is a formal occasion. Ensure that your appearance is neat, clean and tidy. Well-pressed appropriate clothes, polished, clean footwear, etc. are normally expected. The type of dress reflects your personality, values and character. Good grooming will certainly enhance your personality projection. A well-groomed person gives out a message that he/she is thorough, efficient and has high personal standards. Moreover, when you look good, you feel good and when you feel good, you act good.
- Do not fight any of your natural habits. We are creatures of habit. So, if you have formed any simple habits such as having coffee, eating breakfast, exercising, meditation, prayers, etc., try to fit them into your routine on the day of an interview too. This will help you perform better.

After reaching the interview site

- Complete the official formalities (security check, entry in a guest register, etc.).
- Use the washroom to ensure that you are spick and span: hands are clean, hair is in place. Adjust your dress, including tie, scarf, dupatta, belt, shirt, etc. before entering the interview room.

When waiting to be called for the interview

Very often you would be required by the organization to wait with others in an adjoining room/waiting area with the other candidates, before you are called in. You are likely to be tense and nervous at this stage. Here is what you can do:

- Do whatever naturally relaxes you: reading, deep-breathing, meditation, Reiki, etc.
- Think of pleasant experiences; do not fume and fret.
- The waiting time may also be productively used by chatting with other candidates or even representatives of the company to gather vital information about the organization, names of the interviewers, etc.
- Ask for literature, if any, concerning the organization, and study them.
- Practice affirmation and visualization.

The Interview

Entry

Entry is very important. Knock gently and open the door. Before entering the room, enquire by saying, “May I come in Sir/Ma’am?” If they allow you, make sure you shut the door softly behind you, while facing the interviewers. Greet them by warmly wishing them “Good morning/afternoon/evening! My name is...” Walk confidently towards them with a steady gait, without stooping, slouching or being too erect. Smile. This is the best way to:

- disarm the person in front of you
- create a cordial atmosphere
- make the new person take a liking for you

Smiling also reduces your nervousness and makes you more relaxed and positive.

If the members of the interview panel offer their hands, give them a warm, confident, firm handshake accompanied by a smile and eye contact. Do not sit till you are asked to. When asked to sit, politely thank the interviewers and then sit. If the interviewers are standing, wait for them to sit down first before sitting.

All this will create a good first impression of the candidate. And first impressions are lasting, even as they are formed within 30-60 seconds. Remember, you never get a second chance to make a fantastic first impression.

In your entry, the interviewers observe and judge the following things about you:

- Grooming
- Poise
- Gait
- Manners
- Cheerfulness

Body Language

This is being observed. Sit erect, bend forward slightly showing an attitude of interest and attention. Convey a sense of enthusiasm and energy. Do not be laidback. Be 'professionally relaxed'. Do not fiddle with anything: pen, glass, spectacles, other items on the table, handkerchief, tie, etc. Do not fidget by twitching, picking your nose/ears, arm-scratching, twirling your moustache, etc. It shows a lack of confidence and concentration.

Also, do not place your hand/folder on the interviewers' table.

Answering questions

In general, apply the following principles:

- Listen, think and then talk (not the other way around).
- Do not be in a hurry to give answers, take your time. If you have not heard the question clearly, politely ask for a repeat.
- If you do not know the answer, reply politely that you do not know. If it is an important question, say 'no' without using the words 'no' or 'don't know'. Frame your answer in a positive way.
- If you have made a mistake in your answer or observation, admit and accept it.
- Do not bluff. A dishonest person is summarily rejected.
- Be brief in your replies. Nobody likes a verbose person. Be brief without sacrificing clarity, completeness and courtesy.
- Do not lose your cool even if sometimes questions are intimidating or provocative. Remember, it is only a method of judging you. Do not allow yourself to get stressed. Interviewers may deliberately try to provoke you.
- Practice listening skills. Do not interrupt the interviewers.
- Avoid filler words such as 'follow me', 'get me', 'I am trying to say', 'ok', 'you see', 'I mean', 'As a matter of fact', etc.
- Hold the interviewer's attention with eye contact, smile and voice modulation.
- Display enthusiasm, energy and pleasant expressions while answering questions.
- Do not smoke even if they offer you a cigarette (unless of course, you are a very senior person).
- Ideally, politely decline snacks and beverages, if you are offered any.

- Try to lead the interview. Tell the interviewers what you would like them to know about you, your achievements, your aspirations, motivations, etc.
- Ask questions. Interviewers like candidates who ask questions. Enquire about working conditions, growth prospects, working relationships, training, mobility and relocation, clarify information about the job and the company. By these questions, the interviewer will appreciate your keenness and maturity in relation to the job.
- Avoid slang. It may not be understood and certainly not appreciated. An interview is a formal occasion and your communication must be as formal and explicit as possible.
- Be well-mannered and courteous. Lavishly and generously sprinkle words like “Thank you”, “Beg your pardon”, “Yes please”, etc. This reflects your culture and upbringing.
- Be loyal to your last and/or present organization. Never speak against them. This will be an assurance to the interviewer that you would also be loyal to his/ her organization if and when you join them.
- Maintain eye contact throughout the interview. This will not only help in making a personal impact but will also send a message of your integrity, honesty and self-confidence.
- Be natural. Do not adopt any style/accent. It will show that you are genuine and authentic.
- Sell yourself. There is an element of salesmanship in every interview. You are the product. Arouse interest in the interviewer to buy your services at a price which is fair to both you as well as the organization.
- Take care of interviewer’s fatigue. Sometimes, the interviewers are too tired and are not keen on asking

questions or seeking information. In such a situation, you must be proactive and volunteer vital information about yourself, your achievements, etc.

Questions in an interview can be divided into:

- Opening questions
- Technical questions
- Closing questions

Questions may also be classified as:

- Open ended questions
- Close ended questions

Recognize the questions and deal with them appropriately.

No matter what or how many questions the interviewer asks, fundamentally there are only three basic answers being sought:

- Can he/she do the job?
- Will he/she do the job?
- Will he/she fit into my organization?

You must endeavour to give the interviewer positive assurance to the above three questions.

Some frequently asked questions and suggested approaches/answers

Tell me about yourself.

Keep your answer to 1-2 minutes. Do not ramble. This is a general question. You can say almost anything about yourself. Do not repeat or recount what is already in your resume. Tell things which are not mentioned in it such as your traits, special qualities, achievements, aspirations, motivations and ambitions. Match your qualifications, skills and personality to the requirements of the job. Say a lot without being verbose or self-opinionated.

Why should we hire you?

Think. Stress the positive aspects which have attracted you to apply for this position. Do not mention the negative aspects of your current job. Do not adversely criticize your present employers. Be loyal to them.

What motivates you?

Career growth, opportunity to learn new skills, congenial atmosphere, good co-workers.

Why do you want to leave your present job?

This question is asked to ascertain your sense of loyalty. As already explained, never let down your organization or the people who work for it. You may give reasons such as location, salary limitations, the quality of work, or growth aspirations for wanting to leave your present job.

What do you think qualifies you for this position?

I have read your job description and I believe that I have the relevant experience and background to take charge of this position and the responsibilities that go with it.

Why do you wish to work in our organization?

I have met a few people working in your organization and I am impressed by the flexibility the organization offers its people, the opportunity to move from one functional area to another, etc.

Why did you select this particular field?

It intrigues me. I have qualified in it to use my skills and abilities to the desired extent and this is what I can do best with the kind of experience to back me up.

What is most important to you in a job? What would you like to avoid?

The most important thing in a job for me is job satisfaction in terms of executing challenging assignments and producing positive results, thereby enhancing myself professionally. I would like to avoid monotonous work.

What are your strengths?

I am a team player, result-oriented and have strong interpersonal skills and intelligence to take responsibility and carry out tasks through to a closure.

What are your weaknesses?

Do not say that you have no weaknesses. Not one will buy that. It is better to admit to a shortcoming/weakness and talk about what you are doing to overcome it. For example, you can say something like this: "This job requires a fairly high degree of computer savviness. I think I lack computer skills (or I do not have computer skills to the desired extent) and to overcome this shortcoming, I have joined computer classes and I am also taking the help of my friends so that I can acquire the required skills in a short while."

To take another example, you could say, "This job requires the ability to make presentations before a group of people. Public speaking is not my forte and I feel nervous to speak in front of a group. I have, therefore, enrolled for public speaking and personality development courses, and I am confident that in a short while, I will become good at public speaking and will be able to make excellent presentations.

Another approach would be to just say something like this: "I am normally cool, calm and collected but I have a tendency to become impatient sometimes with colleagues/subordinates who dish out mediocre work and fail to meet targets."

How would you describe a typical workday?

A day which is a productive one, where work is planned properly and executed strongly.

What kind of people do you enjoy working with?

I enjoy working with people who are level-headed, share their learnings, co-operate and are friendly.

Describe your present boss in a few words.

An excellent guide and motivator.

What are your salary expectations?

This is a very sensitive question both for the interviewer and the interviewee. Be prepared to face this question. If this question is asked, you should not feel shy or bashful to spell out your expectations. It is your right to discuss your salary expectations. Talk confidently and in a matter-of-fact manner. Be rational and logical about your approximate expectations. For example, if you are currently employed, a 15-20 % increase would be considered as rational. It would be helpful if you enquire from friends or employees of the organization regarding the salary structure and what one could reasonably expect and then pitch your expectations to the interviewer.

You must not limit the discussion to only the salary part. You must also clarify about the kind of benefits the organization gives such as provident fund, bonus, gratuity, pension, leave travel allowance, medical reimbursement, entertainment allowance, interest-free housing loan, etc.

Remember that the discussion on salary is an important one and the right of every interviewee.

Where do you see yourself 5-10 years from now?

This question is aimed at finding out your aspirations. Unrealistic aspirations will indicate that either you have not seriously thought about your aspirations or that you are out of touch with reality. Therefore, think about your aspirations, be realistic and then answer this question.

How do you spend your free time? What are your hobbies?

This is a loaded question as your answer will give a clue to the interviewer about your personality. The principle behind this question is the belief that since time is a scarce commodity, a person would, in his/her spare time, like to do things that are enjoyable and temperamentally suit the person. Thus, if the interviewee says that in his spare time, he reads, paints, cooks, listens to music, etc. it would indicate that he is an introvert, a loner. Such a person will be suitable for a job which requires minimum interaction with other people such as research work, auditing, accounting, etc. On the other hand, there are jobs such as sales, public relations, etc. which require a person with a high degree of interaction and team spirit. Those who appear to be group oriented (participating in games such as football, hockey or indulging in other group activities) are likely to be selected.

Therefore, this question requires that you modify your answer (without bluffing) to suit the job you have applied for.

Why do you consider yourself suitable for this job?
Why should I give this job to you?

To answer this question effectively, it is essential that you prepare yourself well in advance and tailor-make your answer to what the interviewer would like to hear. The company is concerned with whether you have the required knowledge, skills, attitudes and habits for the particular position/job. Your answer should make it abundantly clear that you have them in large measure. Also, drive home that your personality profile, which includes your psychological and emotional make-up, upbringing, values and motivation makes you eminently suitable for the job.

Ending the interview

- Smile. Say a few appropriate words. Thank the interviewers politely and wish them. Shake hands, only if offered — warm, confident, firm handshake.

- Your picking up things, rising from the chair, etc. are observed. These movements will reflect your self-confidence. Do these movements gracefully and elegantly.
- Walk briskly. Open the door while facing the interviewer. Smile and close the door gently behind you after you have stepped out.
- Wait a couple of minutes in the outer office. Perhaps the interviewer may, as an afterthought, wish to ask or clarify something with you.
- Do not forget to wish the secretary or interview coordinator before leaving the office.

Post interview

You can follow up the interview by sending a simple, courteous email or letter to the interviewer thanking him/her for calling you for the interview.

It is important and useful to analyse the highlights of the interview objectively. It is a good idea to jot down all the questions asked and the answers given by you. Three benefits will flow from this:

- It will help you make an objective assessment.
- You can make sure you do not contradict yourself if you are called for a second interview by the same company.
- If you follow this practice with other interviews also, gradually a pattern of questions which are generally asked will emerge.

What qualities do interviewers look for?

What the interviewers look for in candidates differs from

organization to organization and from job to job. However, there are certain common qualities they look for regardless of the job in question. These qualities are:

Personality projection

The type of personality required would differ from job to job. Irrespective of the type of job, all interviewers would certainly like a well-groomed candidate who is pleasant, self-sufficient and confident. An enthusiastic, energetic and sincere person is always preferred.

Communication skills

Communication skills is one of the most important factors all interviewers assess because communication is vital for smooth functioning of any organization. The degree of communication skills required may be different in different jobs. For example, the communication skills required by a person in the kitchen of a 5-star hotel will be different from that of a front office or housekeeping employee in the same hotel. Good communication skills would mean speaking in a pleasant tone, at the right speed, each word articulated correctly and with the right pronunciation and in an appropriately loud voice.

Knowledge

The knowledge of a candidate is one of the key factors in the selection of the candidate. The different kinds of knowledge that the interviewer looks for are.

- Knowledge of the company the candidate is presently working with
- Knowledge pertaining to the post you are undergoing the interview for

- Knowledge of the area of your specialization
- General knowledge of the world and events around you
- Knowledge of yourself in terms of your strengths, weaknesses, values and beliefs

Education and experience

The more relevant the qualifications (education), the greater the chances of being selected. Although higher grades/ marks are preferred, they may not be the sole factor to tilt the balance in a person's favour. The company may prefer a candidate with average academic performance combined with an all-round personality. The higher the reputation of the institute in which the candidate has studied, the greater the chances of success.

Although experience relevant to the job is preferred, frequent changes of jobs is not appreciated or approved of. A job-hopper is viewed with suspicion by interviewers.

Achievements

It is believed that if you have achieved in the past, you will continue to achieve in the future. In other words, you will be achievement oriented. Therefore, all interviewers take a special interest in the achievements of a candidate, whether in school, college or in previous employment.

Personal qualities

Personal qualities are very vital for any job. The interviewee must project his/her best qualities in the interview. The common qualities for all job positions are honesty, commitment and team spirit. Other qualities such as the ability to work under stress, achievement orientation, ability to work long hours doing routine tasks, communication skills, etc. vary for different jobs. For example, an airline pilot would need to be balanced under stress, a research associate would need a high achievement orientation, a salesperson would need to have good oral communication skills whereas an accountant would require the ability to work for long hours at a desk. The interviewer tries to ascertain such qualities in an interview.

Your past or present data present pointers/indicators to the interviewer. Thus, for example, a person who has been school captain is likely to have leadership qualities. A sportsman is likely to be result-oriented and a team-player depending on the game of proficiency. A person engaging in hobbies like fishing, stamp-collecting, listening to music, art, reading, etc. indicates a person who is a loner and is comfortable to be by oneself, whereas a person who participates in group games and social activities is likely to be interpreted as being an outgoing person.

Every candidate must find out the requirements of the job and then in the interview, project these qualities.

Some common reasons for rejection

- Untidy or incomplete resume
- No real interest in the job/organization
- Lack of knowledge
- Lack of past achievements
- Drops names of influential persons
- Uses parent's influence
- Lack of mobility
- Laziness
- Low moral standards
- Non-punctual
- Disorganized, rambling answers

- Superficial answers
- Sloppy candidate
- Bluffing.
- Wrinkled or dirty clothes
- Casual approach
- Overfamiliarity in the interview
- Disrespectful
- Loud voice
- Poor physical projection
- Lack of manners
- Over-emphasis on money rather then on growth prospects
- Aggressive and flashy
- Lack of career plans
- Dishonest
- Over-ambitious
- Lack of tact/diplomacy
- Immaturity
- Unrealistic aspirations
- Condemnation of past bosses/organisations
- Poor communication skills
- Lack of sincerity
- Artificial
- Lack of vitality
- Lack of eye contact
- Feeble handshake
- Disturbed family or marital life

Interview etiquette

Some do's:

- Dress appropriately, keeping in mind the post applied for.
- Reach the venue 10-15 minutes ahead of time. Use this time to freshen up and mentally prepare yourself.
- When called in, exchange pleasantries.
- Maintain direct eye contact but do not overdo it. This will make the interviewer uncomfortable.
- Walk and sit with a good posture.
- Shake hands firmly but briefly.
- Behave in a relaxed manner.
- Smile when you arrive and leave and where appropriate during the interview.
- Speak clearly and loudly enough to be heard.
- Be nice to everyone in the office, not just the interviewer.
- While concluding the interview, be gracious and express your happy feelings for being considered for the job.
- Write a short thank you note after the interview and add something to it that enhances your image — may be one of your strong points that did not come out during the interview.
- Do find out about the company and possibly the interviewer. It will make you feel more comfortable if you know the environment.
- Do make sure that you do not have body odour or bad breath.
- Do get serious about the job and show that you will give 100% commitment to the company.
- Do sound like you have a long-term plan about

yourself and the company

- Do listen to what the interview says about the job and build on that. Ploughing on without taking in what the interviewer says is a real rapport buster.
- Do look at the interviewer as you speak. Otherwise, it will look like you lack confidence or are hiding something.

Some don't's:

- Don't get aggressive or overambitious. Draw a balance.
- Don't be too polite or smile right through. You may give the impression that people can walk all over you.
- Don't give model answers just because they sound right. Lack of sincerity shows, especially when you are talking to professionals experienced in their field.
- Don't criticize another company or person if asked for an opinion. The interviewer may feel you are an unfair person.
- Don't get too familiar with the interviewer. It is best to maintain a no-nonsense attitude, while being polite and pleasant.
- Don't come across as desperate. Nobody wants to hire someone no one else wants.
- Don't ask about fringe benefits, vacations or salary until you have a firm offer.
- Don't chew gum. Don't use slang. Don't use profanity. Don't call the interviewer by the first name. Don't try to be an instant buddy.
- Don't carry huge parcels, large shopping bags or handbags, etc. which make you look burdened down. Enter the interview room only with a small briefcase

or a small handbag. If you have any other extra bags, do not take that to the interview room. Leave them in the reception area.

- Don't accept an offer of coffee or tea. You may spill it on the floor or the table. It is best to politely decline the offer.
- If you are going to be interviewed over lunch or dinner, don't order anything that is difficult to eat. And don't drink anything alcoholic. You need to be at your sharpest.

Chapter 22

DEBATING SKILLS

A group discussion is a collaborative exercise in which a group of persons has a discussion to find out various perspectives. A debate on the other hand, is a competitive situation in which each party tries to prove itself right and the opponent wrong. Whether it is a formal debate where two teams take up sides on a subject/topic or an informal argument between two persons, the aim of a debate is to prove the other wrong or inefficient. Therefore, to excel in a debate, it is necessary that you:

- Present your case forcefully and convincingly.
- Do not contradict yourself and/or change your stand. Stick firmly to your viewpoint.
- Listen attentively to your opponent only with a view to find flaws in his/her argument and to demolish his case. Attack the opponent's ideas and views, not the person himself/herself.
- Use wit, humour, sarcasm to score debating points over the opponent.
- A very important element in debating is the art of attractive and persuasive speech.
- Another important weapon in the debater's armoury is command over language. It enriches and adorns almost every other quality. Most people find pleasure

in hearing their own language spoken with ease and grace. Therefore, develop a sense of literary form — your mind must be stored with the treasures of our great literary inheritances upon which you may draw at will.

- The debater must make use of the right words at the right time.
- The debater must be a student of words. He/she must study master orators and the way they use words powerfully. Use of graceful and simple language, even in casual conversations, is an accomplishment greatly to be desired.
- The whole art of debating consists of presentation — develop the wonderful power of presentation. Captivate your audience in language of the simplest and the most lucid kind. Voice, gesture, knowledge, language, emotion — all go into the art of presentation.
- Simplicity of speech linked with the expression of deep feelings has the power to move people.
- The presentation, above all things, must be orderly.
- The first most important and vital thing is to know your case with complete thoroughness. You must have complete mastery of facts and figures and the power to present them in the most attractive way.
- A debater must have something valuable to say. Eloquence without substance is like a table beautifully set with flowers, but no food!
- A good debater, like a good lawyer, spends more time preparing the opponent's case than one's own. He/she will try to anticipate the opponent's strong points and how he/she will protect himself/herself against them. What are the opponent's weak points? How may one capitalize on those? Likewise, a good debater will be aware of one's own strong points and how those may

be driven home. He/she will also be acutely aware of one's own weaknesses and how to defend and protect his/her case.

- Another important skill is the 'art of transforming disadvantage to victory', or what is known as the ability to make a quick, effective repartee. This is the ability to think on your feet. Have a quick mind; here are a couple of examples demonstrating this point:
    - o Once, Lady Astor told Winston Churchill, "Mr. Churchill, you are so obnoxious that if you were my husband, I would put poison in your coffee." Churchill immediately replied, "And Madam, if I were your husband, I would most willingly drink that coffee."
    - o Two politicians, hostile to each other, found themselves in a small passage. One could not pass if the other did not make way. So, the first politician said, "Please make way for me, I am in a hurry." The second replied, "I do not make way for scoundrels." The first politician, bowing down and moving aside said, "But I do."
    - o A senior statesman once accosted Benjamin Disraeli and shouted, "Mr. Disraeli, you are so unprincipled and such a blackguard that you will either die on the gallows or die of venereal disease." Mr. Disraeli smilingly replied, "That all depends on whether I embrace your principles, or I embrace your mistress."

Unfortunately, most of us are not quick-witted and fail to give a prompt and telling reply when the occasion demands it. As one humourist sadly observed, "I make my repartee after I have made my departee."

- Finally, the effect achieved depends on the character and the quality of the speaker himself. The distinctive quality of personality gives compelling power. All great orators have had this distinctive quality.

- A good debater always remembers that "an educated person is very easy to lead, difficult to drive, easy to govern, impossible to enslave."

Chapter 23

LISTENING

"To be open is to Listen, not only to yourself, but to every influence, to every movement about you."

J. Krishnamurti.

"Nature gave human beings two ears but only one tongue which is a gentle hint that they should listen more than they talk". Listening requires two ears, one for meaning and one for feeling".

Most of us are under the mistaken notion that communication is all about speaking, writing and holding forth. This notion is given an impetus, a reinforcement by the educational system which devotes most of its time and energy to imparting reading and writing skills. People — adults as well as students — are encouraged, motivated to take part in debates, elocution competitions and group discussions. People enrol in public speaking courses and attend writing workshops — but hardly ever anybody teaches us listening skills - there are hardly any courses available on active listening. The truth is that the process of communication has to do more with listening than with speaking. We need to place adequate emphasis on listening skills because we have almost lost touch with the art of listening.

Although we all lay claim to be listening, very few of us actually listen. We are all in so much of a hurry and there is so much noise and chaos in our lives that we are hardly alive to the world around us and to the world within us. We block out so much either because we are in a tearing hurry or because we are too full of ourselves. In the bargain, we fail to "Listen" to opportunities and possibilities which life may offer us.

What is Listening? Listening has been defined by Bernice Hurst [in the Hand Book of Communication Skills] as the "Process of absorbing words and selecting meaning". It has also been described as "the reception of ideas". Listening is not Hearing. As Keith Davies puts it, "Hearing is with the ears but Listening is with the mind". It is not even hearing patiently" — that is only one aspect — not the total process of Listening. Listening is an intellectual activity. Paying attention to the speaker's body language and to non¬verbal messages is part of the process of listening. The success of oral communication depends largely on the effectiveness of the listener. That is why it has been said that "listening is the other half of talking". If people stop listening, it is useless to "talk".

- Listening is an attitude towards other people. Listening is giving close attention with the purpose of hearing in such a way that "Understanding is achieved".

There are two types of content in a Message: -

a. Cognitive ["Factual" Content — this is conveyed by words]

b. Affective ["Feeling" Content — this is conveyed by Body Language, Tone of Voice, Gestures, Facial Expressions — i.e. Non-verbal communication]

Listening means capturing both types of content.

LISTENING IS A POWERFUL, SPECIFIC TOOL TO BUILD UP YOUR INTER¬PERSONAL SKILLS [RELATIONSHIPS].

Listening is a skill — a difficult skill. And like any other skill it can be learned and developed.

IMPORTANCE OF LISTENING

Most people spend more time listening than reading, writing or speaking.

An Ohio University study has revealed that executives spend their time as under: -

9 % - Writing

16 % - Reading

30 % - Speaking

45 % - Listening

Total - 100 %

Thus, out of the four communication skills, listening seems to be the most important. And it is opined that, the higher you climb the Organizational ladder, the more important listening becomes.

REWARDS FOR LISTENING

There are many benefits and rewards of good listening. Some of the rewards are:

1. Increased Job Knowledge / Increased Learning.
2. Broadened Experience.
3. Deeper Friendships.
4. Increased Job Opportunities and Promotions.
5. Helps in Sizing up people — in meetings, new settings, etc.
6. Helps to prevent little grievances from becoming big. Troubles disappear.
7. It is vital to a Manger's success — to work effectively, a manager must first understand worker's feelings, viewpoints, etc.
8. Decision makers who listen well have more information for making sound decisions.

9. It is most vital and useful in the "Helping" professions — Viz. — for Doctors, Psychiatrists, Social workers, counsellors, etc. Also, very essential in Sales, Marketing, Public Relations, Service Industry, Customer Care, etc.
10. Builds up your Professional Image — gives you the reputation of being a courteous person and a good "Conversationalist". People gravitate to those who try to understand their point of view through thoughtful listening.

BARRIERS TO LISTENING

There are many barriers to good listening. These can be classified as "External" barriers and "Internal" barriers

A. EXTERNAL BARRIERS

- Impaired Hearing: - If your hearing is defective, obviously you cannot listen well.
- Fatigue, Lack of Energy: - It is difficult to listen well when you are tired.
- Indisposition — obviously if you are not in good health, it becomes more difficult to listen well.
- Distractions — in the form of Noise, Heat, Glare, etc.
- Interruptions — by people, phone-calls are barriers to good listening
- Late Comers — they are big interruptions and distractions to the process of listening.
- Different people are claiming your attention at the same time — when many people clamour for your attention simultaneously, it is impossible to listen adequately to any one of them.

B. INTERNAL BARRIERS

Good listening is not adversely affected by external barriers alone. Even if we eliminate the external barriers, there are other barriers to good listening. A few stories will be illustrative: -

a) A couple celebrated their Golden Wedding Anniversary on a grand scale. After all the guests had departed, the man turned to his wife and said: "I'm proud of you".

   The Wife replied: "It's alright; I'm tired of you too".

   Thus, frequently, we don't even hear what the other is saying.

b) A reporter was interviewing a woman on her 70th birthday. The woman, who was a spinster, was extraordinarily talented, vivacious and full of energy. The reporter asked the woman: "Have you ever been Bed-ridden". The woman blushed and replied: "Only Twice".

   Thus, we put our own meaning to what is said.

c) A Woman told her husband: "I'm ashamed of the way we live — my father pays our rent, my brother sends food and money for clothes, my uncle pays the water and electricity bills; our friends pay for entertainment, etc. I am not complaining, but really we can do better". And the husband replied. "Of course — you have 2 brothers and an Uncle who don't send us a cent".

   Thus, we hardly ever talk of the same thing.

d) A village drunkard met the local priest. He asked the priest, "what causes Arthritis?"

   The Priest looked at the drunkard contemptuously and replied:

   "Drinking causes Arthritis"

   "Gambling causes Arthritis"

"Chasing loose women causes Arthritis"

After this outburst, the priest turned to the drunkard and said: "But why do you ask this"? and the drunkard replied, "The newspapers say that the Pope has got Arthritis".

Thus, often we don't listen and respond to what we assume the other said.

e) A 14-year old boy was chosen to teach his class the next day. His father was an expert in Instructional Methods. He elementally advised his son to "Choose objectives made of Action, situation and level of performance and that he must give practical demonstration". The boy replied: "It won't work". And the father screamed: "Of course, it will work; I'm an expert and I know it. I've been doing it for 30 years. Why will it not work"? And the boy replied: "I'm supposed to give a class on sex".

Thus, often we don't listen and decide beforehand what the other is talking about.

The five incidents narrated above very clearly illustrate that there are many Internal Barriers to Good Listening. Some of the Internal Barriers are:

1. We prefer things to people. We are more comfortable with files, Papers, mail, etc. They are our comfort zones. We choose them rather than face / confront people and deal with them appropriately.
2. We are basically self-centred; we are only interested in ourselves; we always want to be the centre of Attraction. Therefore, we tend to switch off if the message does not directly and vitally concern us.
3. Our prejudices / our Habit of prejudging people / events — we are full of ourselves; we want to prove others wrong.
4. We are afraid / we avoid listening to a different

viewpoint; we avoid listening to new ideas; we desire to preserve the status quo — we switch off when new ideas are presented.

5. Our tendency to "interrupt". We love to interrupt. We hardly ever allow the speaker to complete his message.
6. We dwell on the inadequacies of the speaker instead of paying attention to his message.
7. Semantic Barriers — words have different meaning for different people. Emotion laden words trigger strong emotions in people which adversely affect Listening.
8. Social Distance / Status Barrier.
9. Passive Indifference — we are involved in doing many things at the same time. Therefore, it's natural that we don't give enough attention to listening — in fact we may become indifferent to it.
10. Lack of interest in subject / topic.
11. Topic/ subject is too easy or elementary for us. In which case, we tend to switch off.
12. Topic / subject is too difficult for us. In which case, after initial attempts at understanding we may give up listening out of frustration.
13. Impatience — we are pushed for time — we tend to hurry the speaker — we start playing with objects which are handy. All this lessens the quality of our listening.
14. Tendency to respond inappropriately — when, for e.g. somebody is in difficulty or trouble and opens up to us, we give a comforting response or a "Motivating / Encouraging" response. This is not helpful. What is really required is an "empathetic" response. We must see the situation with his eyes, with his mind and from

his view point and help him get in touch with his real feelings. This will empower him to deal adequately with his situation / problem.

15. The Root Cause for poor listening is the wide gap between speaking speed and comprehension speed. A person, at an average, speaks about 125 to 150 words per minute whereas the human brain has the capacity to comprehend 500 to 600 words per minute. In this gap, the mind loafs — it wanders away from the topic / subject. If we can gainfully utilize this time — say, for e.g. by listening to the non-verbal communication of the speaker, or by paraphrasing the speaker's message in our mind — we will become good, active listeners.

In conclusion it can be summed up by saying: "If I do not interrupt; if I avoid distracting actions; if I am my natural self; if I paraphrase in my mind; If I seek clarification at the appropriate time, I am an effective listener".

We give below a "creative" description of "Good Listening"

L LOOK INTERESTED

Show encouragement by

Facing the speaker

Keeping eye contact

Staying relaxed

Leaning forward slightly

Maintaining an open posture

I INQUIRE WITH QUESTIONS

Clarify the speaker's meaning

Ensure you get the full story

Remember the various types of questions open to you

S STAY ON TARGET

Stick to the point — remember your purpose

Listen for the central theme of what is being said

Think ahead

Wait for the complete message. Don't prejudge.

Don't 'yes but ......' Be patient

T TEST YOUR UNDERSTANDING

Ensure you really do understand what the speaker is saying

Restate to make sure 'So what you're saying is.....'

E EVALUATE THE MESSAGE

Identify the speaker's purpose

Analyse what is said

Reasoning

Flaws or fallacies?

Generalization?

Causes linked to effects?

Emotional appeal?

Evidence

Facts or assertions?

Complete or Partial?

Information source?

Up-to-date? Reliable?

Language

Use of unfamiliar words? Jargon?

Body language? Consistent with verbal message?

Voice related indicators

Tone

Pitch

Speed of delivery

N NEUTRALISE YOUR FEELINGS

Stay calm. Retain self-control

Don't get heated or emotional

Keep an open mind.

SUGGESTIONS FOR EFFECTIVE LISTENING

- STOP TALKING

  You cannot listen if you are talking.
  Polonius (Hamlet): "Give every man thine ear, but few thy voice".

- PUT THE TALKER AT EASE.

  Help a person feel free to talk
  This is often called a permissive environment.

- SHOW A TALKER THAT YOU WANT TO LISTEN.

  Look and act interested. Do not read your mail while someone talks.
  Listen to understand rather than to oppose.

- REMOVE DISTRACTIONS.

  Don't doodle, tap, or shuffle papers.
  Will it be quieter if you shut the door?

- EMPATHIZE WITH TALKER

  Try to help yourself see the other person's point of view.

- BE PATIENT.

  Allow plenty of time. Do not interrupt a talker.
  Don't start for the door or walk away.

- HOLD YOUR TEMPER.

  An angry person takes the wrong meaning from words.

- GO EASY ON ARGUMENT AND CRITICISM.

  These put people on the defensive, and they may become angry or 'Clam up'.
  Do not argue: Even if you win, you lose.

- ASK QUESTIONS.

  This encourages a talker and shows that you are listening.
  It helps to develop points further.

- STOP TALKING.

  This is first and last, because all other guides depend on it. You cannot do an effective listening job while you are talking.

Chapter 24

AFFIRMATION AND VISUALIZATION

An affirmation is a positive declaration of what you want to be, what you want to have or how you want to live, as if it is already so. In other words, an affirmation is a statement that describes a goal in its completed state. The essence of the efficacy of affirmations is to fill your subconscious mind with new powerful thoughts and images of things like enjoying health, wealth, exciting vacations, fulfilling relationships, etc. — essentially, of all your goals as already achieved or completed.

An affirmation is a controlled and directed self-talk which gives direction and impact to your plans and goals for health, wealth, self-improvement, etc. and results in higher utilization of your potential. Affirmations transform your thinking, your attitude and finally your behaviour and help to produce the results you desire. It is the fuel for rapid change, the sustenance of self-direction.

Affirmation is known by various names — auto-suggestion, self-talk, self-command, self-motivation, etc.

Why do affirmations work?

The subconscious mind does not distinguish between truth and falsehood. It accepts everything you say to it as an order and says 'Yes' to the order. It actually works to produce what you have ordered. The repetition of positive thoughts over and over, day after day, begins to affect your subconscious mind — the creative power within you.

If you keep feeding things to the brain, it remembers and transfers them to the body. Constant repetition produces acceptance and finally, belief. Then, magic happens, and the subconscious mind delivers what you asked for, unconditionally.

Repetition is an infallible technique of making the mind believe and act upon new ideas. You live up to what you expect for yourself. Your affirmation becomes a self-fulfilling prophecy. Therefore, the use of affirmation is a dynamic tool for personal development.

According to Norman Vincent Peale, "When the mental picture is strongly enough held, it actually seems to control conditions and circumstances." Dr. Emile Coue, the French physician of the late 19th century, told his patients that they would improve faster if they adopted the plan of saying over and over, "Every day, in every way, I am getting better and better." Those patients who followed his method found that it worked in spite of the ridicule of others.

With the constant use of affirmations, the law of displacement starts working, i.e., the affirmed ideas replace the earlier conditioning; because you expect to see positive changes, you act in the manner you have affirmed. You become a changed personality because you act according to the expectation you set for yourself.

Affirmations are powerful in bringing about personality change and success. They give a powerful burst of physical energy that energises you in the achievement of goals that are important to you.

Guidelines for constructing effective affirmations

Use personal pronoun 'I'

For more effectiveness, it is recommended that you include your full name in every affirmation. For example, "I, (full name) am happy, healthy and energetic." It is crucial that you use the words "I am", which, according to Jack Canfield, are "the two most powerful words in the language."

Use the present tense

Affirm that something is happening here and now. State what you want as though you already have it. For example, affirm 'I am competent' and not "I am going to be competent."

Be positive

Use only positive words. Always state your affirmations in the most positive terms. Never use negatives in affirmations. Affirm what you do want and not what you don't want.

Wrong: "I am not obese."

Right: "I am slim and trim."

Keep it brief

In general, the shorter and simpler the affirmation, the more effective it is.

Make it specific

Do not be vague. State specifically what you want. For example, don't affirm "I own a car." Instead, affirm "I now own a red, 2015 model Maruti car."

Add a feeling or emotion word

Express an emotion you would feel if you had already achieved your goal. Thus, instead of affirming "I now maintain my ideal weight of 68 Kgs", it is more effective to affirm "I feel proud and happy at my ideal weight of 68 Kgs."

Belief

Believe what you say is happening. The more you believe,

the more powerful and effective is the affirmation.

Always choose affirmations that feel totally right for you

Choose or select or create your own affirmation with which you are most comfortable, and which works best for you because what works for one may not work at all for another.

Repeat

Repetition produces results. Say your affirmations as often as possible. Write it down a few times every morning and evening. Record and play them back. Paste them on notes around your house.

Method of using affirmations

Affirmations can be done silently, spoken out loud, written down or even sung or chanted.

Affirmations must be used repeatedly every day. Repeat them as often as possible. The more, the better. The more you affirm, the faster will be the result. The best times to say your affirmations are:

- The first thing in the morning as soon as you wake up
- The last thing at night before you go to sleep

However, don't restrict yourself to these two times. You can, rather, you should, repeat your affirmation any time during the day or throughout the day.

Finally, write down your affirmations repeatedly for reinforcement.

Visualization

Visualization is another useful technique for focusing your creative power on achieving goals. Visualization is the act of mentally picturing ideas, events, circumstances and objects. The art of visualization enables us to move from the area of dreams to the hard light of reality.

Visualisation is effective in enhancing one's ability to achieve. It is exercised by successful high achievers in every profession.

Like in affirmations, research has shown that visualization improves healing, rejuvenation and also slows down the physical effects of aging. Research has further shown that visualization can produce changes in the body.

Many professional athletes and sportspersons find visualization to be a powerful tool to enhance their athletic prowess.

Why does visualization work?

Your subconscious mind does not differentiate between actual scenes and those you imagine. When you see yourself acting in a certain way, you begin to believe that it is your habitual performance and therefore, it manifests. Your mind talks to your body by using mental images. This dialogue is going on all the time, sometimes in healing ways, sometimes in harmful ways, although much of the time you may not be consciously aware of it. Likewise, your conscious and unconscious mind communicate with each other by using imagery or visualization.

When you see a vivid picture of yourself in possession of your goals, the picture stimulates desire, sparks creativity in planning action steps and fuels motivation to take action. With conscious practice, you can turn the practice and skill of visualization into a powerful habit to improve results and achieve your goals.

To practice visualization, use the following steps:

- Shut your eyes and imagine that you are in possession of what you desire to possess or attain. For example, if you desire to own a car, imagine that you own one and are driving it. Imagine it vividly, colours and all.

- In addition, cut out a picture of the car and paste it, for example, on the bathroom mirror or any other place where you are likely to see it every day.

Visualisation changes a general idea into something more specific. It focuses attention on goals. It increases desires. It intensifies beliefs and commitments. It sharpens concentration and relieves stress. Visualisation fuels motivation.

In conclusion, we may say:

Thought creates after its kind.
Thought attracts that upon which it is directed.
What we think is what we become.
Everything is created twice, first in the mind and then in the physical world.

In the words of Paul Myers:

Whatever you vividly imagine, ardently desire, sincerely believe, and enthusiastically act upon,
Must inevitably come to pass.

By applying the two techniques of affirmation and visualization, you can attain whatever you want and achieve your goals.

Chapter 25

PROFESSIONALISM AND CORPORATE ETIQUETTE

It is important to conduct yourself professionally in your Corporate Life.

Professionalism is "Image Positioning". You are a product. You need to position yourself appropriately. Increase in professionalism leads to an increase in believability, credibility and authenticity. This, in turn, leads to increase in marketability and, finally, in Revenue. Ultimately, professionalism helps you to earn more money.

Professionalism is displayed both by your attitude to your job and your conduct and behaviour at the workplace. It is reflected by, among other things, the following: -

1. **Grooming:** - It is essential to strictly adhere to the Dress-Code laid down by the corporate. If no dress-code has been prescribed, ensure that you are appropriately groomed befitting your position / responsibility in the Organization. Good grooming will boost up your self-image which, in turn, will enhance your Corporate Image.
2. **Appropriate Body Language:** - The way you sit, stand, greet visitors, etc. are very important. They help you to project a good image of yourself. Your body language must always display energy, enthusiasm and

vibrancy. It should always convey a willingness to help, to serve, to take charge, etc.

3. **Punctuality: -** Punctuality is the hallmark of a thoroughbred professional. Punctuality should be displayed at all times — at the start of the Day; after coffee-break, Lunch-break, starting and ending meetings, etc. Punctuality also develops your likeability.
4. **Focus -** A professional is completely focused on the Job. Do not permit yourself to be distracted. During corporate hours, do not deal with or indulge in personal work.
5. **Professional Communication:** Be very professional in your verbal communication — both Oral and Written. Avoid Slang /foul & loose language; maintain proper dignity and decorum in dealing with colleagues, customers, outsiders, etc. Use professional words in your communication. Also, conduct yourself professionally on the telephone. Maintain proper telephonic communication and telephone etiquette. "
6. **Be a good Team Player**
7. **Fulfil your Commitments: -** Deliver what you promise. In fact, endeavour to deliver more than what you promise. But never, never deliver less than what you have promised.
8. **Knowledge -** Acquire and display adequate Product / Technical knowledge.
9. **Sales Service: -** Endevour to make buying a pleasurable experience for the customer followed by good after sales service.
10. **Be Objective: -** Do not allow personal likes / dislikes to influence your corporate decisions. Treat issues on merits and not on whims and fancies.

Professional Conduct and Behaviour in Corporation.

Every work place has its own complex dynamics but there is a certain basic behaviour and conduct which helps an office to function with minimum anxiety and stress. Therefore: -

A. Set Standards:

All behaviour tends to be reciprocative. When you are professional and considerate towards others, you are, in turn, encouraging them to behave in a professional and considerate manner towards you. Thus, it is important you take care to:

- Be Punctual.
- Maintain good attendance record — obtain prior permission to be on leave and in case of an emergency, inform superiors by telephone/SMS that you are going to be absent/coming late, etc.
- Carry your share of the load — you are paid for it.
- Be trust worthy — maintain confidentiality.
- Be careful of whom and what you talk on the phone because there may be people around you who might find your conversation on the phone useful to their interests.
- Maintain neatness and tidiness in office. Untidiness creates bad impression on customers. It also spoils the corporate image. Further, it can offend fellow employees and also cause inefficiency.

B. Men & Women Working Together:

When working together, men and women should regard their working relationship as primary and difference in gender as incidental. Men and Women should be professional, and business-like in their dealings with one another. Men should not have a patronizing attitude towards women nor should they consider women not competent enough purely on the basis of gender. In other words, they should abandon stereotypical thinking on this matter.

A man may extend some special courtesies, like opening the door for a woman or picking up things, etc., these courtesies should be limited to civil behaviour. Thus, a woman's idea should not be given special consideration just because she is a woman. In the same vein it should not be rejected for the same reason. A woman is expected to carry her own share of work and should not expect any special consideration in this regard.

Women should not appeal to male boss's compassion for leaving early on account of sick child / other domestic responsibilities. She should take entitled leave without elaboration upon her domestic problems to her male colleagues. Women should not use seductive behaviour in their dealing with office associates. When a male boss criticizes a woman, her performance / work, she should not get unnecessarily upset about it.

It is both unprofessional and bad manners for a man to make loose comments on the dress or jewellery worn by women. It is also improper and unprofessional to flaunt familiarity with women to others, as people tend to gossip about women. There are some borders / limits across which no professional should stray, most obvious of which are: -

- Touching someone deliberately.
- Making lascivious remarks to or about a lady.
- Staring at a female employee or eyeing her up and down.
- Singing or humming songs at women.

OFFICE FRIENDSHIPS:

1. At work place where attractive, intelligent and

ambitious men and women work together in close contact all day, it is quite possible that friendships may develop into closer, more personal relationships.

2. In this, there is no lack of professionalism or breach of office etiquette as long as friendship does not affect the standard of work and does not affect office decorum and dignity during the working day.
3. However, when employees conduct personal friendships during office time, they are guilty of unprofessional behaviour, poor manners and questionable judgment.

Professional Conduct towards Superiors in Office:

- Be punctual and polite. Smile a lot, dress decently and never neglect the opportunity to say "Please", "Thank You", "Sorry, "Welcome", etc.
- Know your superior's style of functioning and adjust accordingly. ;
- Know your superior's organizational priorities and keep your work up to date.

Be prepared with information that you think he may need.

- Do not gossip to him about your colleagues or spread rumours.
- Be a team player and help wherever and whenever you can.
- Do not pass on office information, process or ideas to people outside the office.
- Always enter your Boss's cabin / Table with pen / Pencil and writing pad to note down the instructions immediately.

Professional Conduct towards Sub-ordinates in Office:

1. Treat Sub-ordinates with courtesy and respect and yet get things done in the most appropriate way.
2. Request rather than command. Give clear instructions.
3. Trust your sub-ordinates — do not give the impression that you are closely watching the work and performance of your juniors.
4. If your superior talks adversely about your sub-ordinate, do not immediately respond. Talk to your sub-ordinate for his side of the story and then act appropriately.
5. If your junior confides in you about his personal problems, do not violate the confidence reposed in you. Respect the confidence placed in you.
6. Never discuss one sub-ordinate, his performance or personality with another. It is both unprofessional and also discourteous to the employee being discussed.
7. Criticize gently. Criticism should be tempered with good manners and consideration for the other person's feelings. Try and make the criticism a learning experience for the sub-ordinates.
8. Do all criticizing in private so that the sub-ordinate is not embarrassed. Do praise in public.
9. Avoid using belittling words like "Fool", "Stupid", "Crazy", Dumb", etc.
10. When reviewing the sub-ordinate's work, the superior must mention the good points first and compliment him if possible. He must then be specific as to what went wrong and how it must be done.
11. In case of a conflict with a sub-ordinate, the superior should maintain a dignity that befits his position and

level in the organization and he should not try to match the sub-ordinate's bad manners with his own.

Conducting Meetings in a Professional Manner:

- Ensure comfortable seating arrangement and adequate papers/stationery, etc. for all those attending the meeting.
- Come prepared for the meeting. Study the relevant papers thoroughly. Do your homework well so that you can contribute meaningfully at the meeting.
- Be punctual — start and end the meeting on time.
- Wish / Greet other members.
- Be polite. Do not raise your voice. Don't speak when another is speaking.
- Avoid sub-grouping.
- Don't dominate the discussions and do not allow anyone else to dominate. Give all members a chance to contribute and interact.
- Maintain eye-contact.
- Listen to others - it is good manners and very professional behaviour.
- Stick to the point under discussion. Don't stray away. And if others have strayed away and taken the discussion off-track, then bring others gently back without being rude.
- Maintain decorum and respect even if you don't agree with the views expressed.
- Do not throw papers, napkins or crumbs of eatables on the floor — keep them aside separately.
- It is both impolite and unprofessional to make noises when eating or drinking.

WHAT NOT TO DO AT MEETINGS:

- Don’t arrive late.
- Don’t open on a comic note and don’t encourage levity.
- Don’t come unprepared.
- Don’t allow telephone or other interruptions.
- Don’t resent questions.
- Don’t discourage discussions.
- Don’t monopolize the meeting. Allow others to express their views and ideas.
- Don’t lose your temper or your control.

Professional Conduct towards Guests / Visitors in Office:

- Men should always rise to greet any visitors, male or female, from outside the Organization. However, a senior officer may choose not to rise to greet male or female junior officers.
- A woman who receives guests may not stand when she has a visitor, but it is a courteous gesture if she stands for a visitor from outside the Organization.

Shaking hands with the Guest:

- A man always shakes hand with men.
- A woman may or may not extend her hand to men.
- The person being visited usually indicates where the guests should sit and takes his seat after the guests are seated.
- If you are a smoker, it would be good manners if you refrain from smoking if your guest is an elderly person

or a lady.

When the Guest Leaves:

- When the guest is about to leave, men should stand and usually shake hands if the guest is a man.
- The man may escort the guest to the door and open the door for him.
- A lady may walk to the door with the guest but usually does not open the door for a man.
- When the guest does not realize that he has taken too much time there is no need to be rude to him. Instead, it can be made politely obvious that you consider the discussion to be over or you could say something like: "This has been a fruitful discussion, thank you very much for coming".

If the guest still does not take the hint, some excuse could be made of a busy schedule.

Chapter 26

EFFECTIVE TELEPHONE MANAGEMENT & TELEPHONE MANNERS!

Telephone Communication is a very important form of Oral Communication. These are days of tele-marketing and tele-interviewing. Most of us have to use the telephone at work either to respond to other people's enquiries or to obtain information from others. Very often the telephone is the only point of contact and will therefore affect the way in which your organization is seen. When you talk on the phone, you are the single representative of your company. Your Company will be judged by the way you talk on the phone. The Process does not stop with the telephone Operator or Receptionist. It continues with all of us - [From the Chairman to the Watchman]. Whenever we talk on the telephone, First Impression is the Last Impression you create on the phone.

Telephone Communication suffers from a few handicaps: -

a) Lack of Physical presence —therefore full force of personality cannot be brought into play.

b) Failure because of Physical defects — wrong transmissions, disturbances, etc. in Communication Line.

c) Failure because of fault of speech. Speech, if not clear

can lead to confusion say for e.g. between “nine” and “five”.

d) Since speakers do not see each other there is a temptation to deal with other things. This tendency must be avoided.

Questions you must ask yourself when using the phone: -

Am I friendly?
Am I Helpful?
Am I efficient?
Do I sound or does my voice sound: Pleasant?
Charming?
Enthusiastic?
Energetic?

OR

Do I sound or does my voice sound: Weak?
Tired? Irritated?
Bored?

Guidelines for both Caller/Receiver

1) Caller must greet receiver and reveal his identity at once.
2) Same with Receiver.
3) End conversation by exchanging pleasantries, courteous words.
4) Good manners to let seniors ring off first.
5) Between buyers and Sellers, customers should be allowed to ring off.
6) On phone, never be verbose. Be simple and brief and concise.
7) Be crisp, clear and ensure that a brief summary of the conversation is done by either party, at the end to increase accuracy of information / ideas being

transmitted.

8) Remember that your tone, voice and language convey all that you wish to convey in a phone conversation. Therefore, minimize actions, gestures, hand and leg movements and concentrate on the quality of verbal communication and be polite. The quality of your voice and your ability to express yourself clearly is most important.

9) Smile on the phone; Smile will make your voice pleasant and soft. It will improve the quality of your voice — will help to create rapport.

10) Familiarize yourself with the features, facilities and options available in your telephone instrument. This will help to increase your efficiency and ensure you are not caught unawares. E.g. transfer of calls, conferencing facility, hold-on, single digit code dialling, etc.

11) Have a good knowledge of your organization, its products and services and your colleagues, job descriptions, functional responsibilities, sections/ depts, etc. This is most essential. It will improve your efficiency on the phone.

12) Remember, most telephone instruments have very sensitive receivers. Therefore, avoid sharing irrelevant comments / remarks with colleagues while on the phone as they may be heard by receiver on the other side and you may be misunderstood and the corporate image may get tarnished.

13) After the conversation don't bang the phone down. It is rude. Put the phone down gently.

14) Don't shout when talking long distance. It will only distort message.

15) When 2nd phone rings while you are on one — ask the 2nd caller if he could wait—but don't have him

waiting endlessly - You may suggest that you would return the call.

16) If you are interrupted while you are speaking on the phone — this should happen only in an extreme urgency — try to finish your call. If you can't, apologize to the person on the other end for the delay for waiting or if the delay is anticipated to be long, say you will call back.
17) Should you pick up an extension and discover you have interrupted a conversation, quickly say "I am sorry" and hang up. It is impolite to listen to other people's conversation.
18) When asked for an appointment on phone — be specific in your reply. Say "you are welcome at...........on.............. "Don't reply that he is free to come in at any time.
19) In office calls, be professional — Don't say "Dear", etc.

Guidelines for the person making Telephone Call

1. Prepare thoroughly before you make a telephone call:
   a) Identify the purpose of the call clearly.
   b) If there are several topics to be covered, it is wise to list them so that you don't miss any point.
   c) Consider the time of the day — for half rates, etc.
   d) Keep the Convenience of the receiver in mind — lengthy call at 5.00 p.m. on Friday evening will not be well received. For international calls — keep time difference in mind.
   e) Before making a call, collect and keep ready any papers, brochures/price-list, etc. that might be required— shows value/consideration for others'

time. Keep pencil/ pad ready — Don't say "hold on" and start looking for pencil/pad.

f) Keep your phone free — don't dial continuously.

2. Avoid making calls in presence of customers or guests calling on you, unless they are pertinent to the business being discussed. It is impolite and discourteous to make a call on some other matter when you are talking to a customer — apart from this you might reveal confidential information when you talk in the presence of others.
3. When you are calling long distance from someone else's phone, pay for the call or at least offer to cover the expenses.
4. If you leave a message with somebody, check his or her name to ensure a proper reference later on if necessary. In case you leave a message in a voice-mail mode or leave a taped message, be specific and to the point.
5. From office — don't call intimate friends at their workplace and say, "Guess Who?" — It may create embarrassment.

Guidelines for the person Receiving Telephone Calls

1. Pick up the telephone before 3rd/4th ring and immediately identify yourself by name/name of organization or dept. Greet the caller suitably.
2. When you pick up the phone, don't say "who is calling?" "Who is this?", instead, say "Who am I speaking to sir/madam?" "May I know who I am speaking to?"
3. You may give special greetings during festivals.

4. When the person required is not available, make an offer to help the caller in any way you can.
5. In corporate situation, don't say "I'll do it" — instead, say" I'll have it done immediately sir"
6. Don't keep caller waiting for an unduly long time for his required information — if necessary, tell him you will call back and then do call back. Give the caller/ customer the option. If he opts to "hold on", don't keep him "holding on" for more than 30 to 35 seconds, keep referring back to him and renew the options.
7. Courtesy demands that we allow the caller/customer his privacy and not persist on knowing who he is [if he is unwilling to give his name].
8. In the case of wrong numbers — be polite to the person calling. Showing annoyance is rude and uncalled for; don't ask for the caller's number in this case.
9. When a call is diverted to you in another person's office, ask your associate's permission to use his telephone and be very brief.
10. Offer alternatives e.g. "Would you like to hold on, or shall I call you back?" Caller can then decide for himself.
11. Keep Caller Informed: If for any reason, you have to leave the Caller on hold, it is crucial that you keep him informed of what is happening — tell him how long you will be and, if appropriate, offer to call him back.
12. Never hold 2 conversations simultaneously. Caller deserves your sole attention — so try to ignore everything else.
13. Transferring calls:
    a) If you have to transfer a call, inform the caller of what is happening. Give him name and extension

number of the person he is being transferred to, so that if he is cut off, he can get right back to the required person.

b) When you get connected to the person you wish to transfer the call to, give him relevant information so that he can deal adequately with the situation.

c) If the person you wish to transfer the call to is engaged or not available, you should give caller options—hold or leave a message.

d) If the caller opts to hold, constantly inform him of the status of proceedings.

14. Taking messages: Messages should be passed on properly and should be acted upon. Commitments must be kept. Otherwise, the caller is left with the impression of inefficiency. Use a suitable message pad. Also make sure that the person you are passing the message on to can read your handwriting. Leave message in a prominent place, where it will be noticed. Avoid just adding messages to someone's "In" Tray. It may get lost beneath Incoming Mail.

Some organizations have "Message Boards" in each dept. or section — Messages can be pinned up. Offering to take a message is the lowest form of help. Offer to do this only after you have explored all other avenues.

When answering someone else's call, instead of saying "Can I take a message?" say: "Can I help at all, or in any way?" And very often you can; then the call is dealt with then and there.

Finally, the most important thing is to treat callers, as you would like to be treated —politely and efficiently.

TELEPHONE HANDLING

	Avoid Casual Words	*Use Professional Words*
	Don't say	***Instead say***
1.	*Don't Forget*	*Please do remember*
2	*Don't hesitate*	*Please feel free*
3	*What's your problem?*	*May I know what your concern is?*
4	*No problem*	*My pleasure*
5	*Free*	*Complementary/No Charge*
6	*Discount*	*Rebate*
7	*One Sec*	*Just a moment please*
8	*Cost*	*Price/Value*
9	*We can't do that*	*What we can do for you is…………*
10	*I'll try*	*I'll do my level best*
11	*I don't know*	*Let me check/I am not too sure*
12	*Yeah*	*Yes sir. That's right*
13	*O.K*	*Very Well sir*
14	*Don't worry*	*Rest assured*
15	*It's Policy*	*That's the procedure, Sir.*
16	*You have to……………*	*You can…………………*
17	*Unfortunately/But/Sadly*	*However*
18	*Sure*	*Certainly*
19	*What is your name? / Who is calling?*	*May I have your name please?*
20	*What do you want?*	*Sorry, I did not catch your last point*
21	*What do you mean?*	*Would you mind repeating it? It sounds important.*

Avoid	***Instead say***
Not on her seat/Not come in yet	*Not at his/her Desk*
Do not know when he / she will come back	*Can I ask her/him to call you back?*
Do not know where he/she is	*Can I assist you?*
Yeah; O.K.; Right, oh!	*Yes sir; Alright sir*
Don't be funny	*Good-Bye!*

A few more hints/suggestions

1) Opening an interaction: Please, in a sense, "see" the customer/another person over the phone. A person calling us "sees" us emotionally just as clearly as if those people were sitting across the table.

2) a) Smile when you talk: Smile gives you confidence and projects an "I am Positive' image. When you smile on telephone, you are in control of your communication. You cannot be angry, afraid, or express any negative emotion while you are smiling.

   b) Speak slowly on the phone: Speak at your normal speed — same rate you would talk if the person were seated across from you. This suggests: "I am confident;" "I am in control", it increases efficiency. Fast talking over phone wastes time; makes it necessary to repeat message — also may result in being connected with wrong person/dept.

3) Pass messages directly to the recipient.

4) Remember that your own reputation and Image of organization will suffer if expected follow-up is slow in coming or not forthcoming at all.

5) If you cannot deal with a Customer's enquiry, record details and agree to a time to call back. And ensure it does happen.

6) If you do have to transfer a call, give details of the Customer and problem to the recipient.

7) Conversely if you are the recipient of such a call, ask the relevant details before beginning conversation with Customer.

8) If transferee does not want to talk to customer, be discreet/tactful: a) Mr. S is not at his desk right now! May I take his message? b) Mr. S is in a meeting. Can I help you? c) I am Sorry, Mr. ……. is not at his desk. Can I ask him to call you back?

9) When you are face to face with a Customer and the phone rings: -

To Customer: Sir, can you wait while I answer?

To Caller: Sir, I am with a Customer. I'll phone you back within ………..or you call me back. Which do you prefer?

Key: The person who is first takes precedence. If you give preference to Customer who phones, you create a barrier between you and the Walk-in Customer.

Try and give the Caller a specific time when you will call back. This will avoid two potential problems: -

a) Caller sitting by the phone like a prisoner.

b) Caller phoning back when it's inconvenient for you.

If the caller says it's an emergency, ask permission form walk-in Customer. Key: First come/First Served.

Some Don't's

1) Do not let the emotions of your previous call influence the present call.
2) Don't take complaints personally.
3) Do not keep any evidence of hurry, worry, annoyance or boredom in your voice.
4) Never hold 2 conversations simultaneously.
5) Do not keep the caller waiting on the line indefinitely or unnecessarily.

Chapter 27

ETIQUETTE DURING INTRODUCTIONS

To avoid situations where neither of the persons introduced catches the other's name, a few points must be noted:

- When introducing people, pronounce names and surnames slowly and coherently.
- Toss in a remark or two about the person(s) you have just introduced. For instance, profession, name of the organization, hobbies, etc. are safe conversational openers.
- Encourage the introduced persons to converse among themselves.

Golden rules of introducing people

- Always address a gentleman to a lady first, never vice versa.
- When introducing two persons of the same sex, the younger of the two must be introduced to the older one.
- Similarly, a young girl must be introduced to a married lady, except if the young lady comes from a high social milieu.

Formal introductions

An introduction consists of presenting a person of lesser importance to a person of greater importance. Business introductions always have a purpose; thus, added information should follow the main introduction.

Rules of introduction

If there is a hierarchy between two persons, always introduce the junior to the senior. If the element of the hierarchy is absent, then introduce the younger person to the older one.

While introducing a man and a woman, it is always the man who is presented to the woman and never the other way around. Exceptions are made when there is an element of direct control between the man and the woman, and the man is the immediate superior of the woman. In such a case, the woman may be introduced to the man.

Self-introductions

- Men, when introducing themselves to each other, do not use titles such as "Mr." However, when they are introducing themselves to women, they may use their title.
- Similarly, women may use their title "Mrs.", "Ms." or "Miss" when introducing themselves to others.
- Self-introductions in business circles are never made by the first names. Either the full name or the last name is used.

How to acknowledge introductions

- Men usually acknowledge introductions by shaking hands as well as verbally. Normally, it is sufficient to say, “How do you do?” This could be followed by some conversation, taking a cue from any additional information given by the introducer.

- “Pleased to meet you” is a standard form of response to an introduction. Nowadays, a plain ‘hello’ or ‘how do you do’ are the accepted forms of response to an introduction. This may be accompanied by a warm handshake. In case you have heard of the person before and have been looking forward to meeting him or her, then say so. It will please the person immensely and endear you to him or her.
- Men in India traditionally do not extend their hand to women for a handshake, but if a woman extends her hand, the man should invariably shake hands with her (not doing so will be regarded as ill-mannered and impolite). The same will be the case in younger/older and hierarchically junior/senior positions.
- Men normally stand to acknowledge introductions. The only exceptions could be when junior executives are being introduced, the senior manager may not stand up.
- Women may or may not stand up to acknowledge introductions, but it is courteous to stand up before a very senior executive or an elderly person.

First names

In today’s informal world, one of the informal habits in vogue is the use of first names in addressing people. But remember to notice how the person is being called or would like to be called. Using first name without invitation will indicate that you are too pushy. The suggestion to use first names should come from the older person or one of the higher rank, if hierarchy is involved. Politeness also demands that a man wait for the lady to initiate the use of first names.

When not to introduce

- One need not introduce people who show disinclination or are not likely to care about being acquainted with each other.
- Certain places or occasions are not conducive for introductions. For instance, when strolling or jogging down the lane with a friend, you meet another and exchange remarks, you need not introduce the two if your exchange lasts for just about a minute or so.

Chapter 28

TABLE MANNERS AND FOOD ETIQUETTE

Let us begin right away with the basics:

- Do not speak with food in the mouth (if spoken to, hold the speaker back with a gesture of your palm, chew food and then talk).
- Do not make noise while eating or drinking.
- Chew food with your mouth closed.
- Always cover your mouth when using a toothpick.
- If starters are served with toothpicks, do not leave the toothpicks on the serving plate.
- Use napkin to clean your lips before sipping from a glass.
- Handling cutlery: The knife must be held in the right hand and the fork in the left. The food is conveyed to the mouth with the help of the fork. Never put knife in the mouth.
- If you are using your fingers to eat, ensure that you do not soil your fingers above the first knuckle.

Sitting down

During a formal meal, sit down with the least possible

noise and chatter. Once seated, stay in a fairly erect posture—not stiff, but not slouched either. Elbows must be close to sides to avoid jabbing your neighbours.

Table chatter

Talk to the person on your right and left and those directly in front of you. To ignore them is very impolite. Do not chat incessantly. Avoid delicate subjects like religion, illness, and politics. Do not be loud while talking.

Refusing a dish

A dish can always be declined with a polite 'No, thank you". However, it is not considered good manners to refuse a dish unless it is for a medical or religious reason, or for a general matter of principle (such as vegetarianism). It is good manners to take a little bit of every dish doing the rounds.

Buffet

Do not make a dash. Avoid jumping queues. Avoid obscenely loading your plate with food — it is far better to go for a second/third helping.

Burping

At a large, formal meal, if there is a hint of an oncoming burp, cover your mouth with a napkin and say, 'excuse me', to no one in particular. In a small, informal group of friends, teasing or joking may take place.

Chewing paan

People sometimes have paan (a betel-leaf preparation) for

therapeutic reasons as well as because they enjoy the taste. Some do it by force of habit. Chewing paan in itself is not unattractive, if it is done quietly and unobtrusively. But doing it with grimaces, open mouth, smacks and crackles is in very bad taste. Worse still, is the habit of spitting. If you feel the need to spit out, please do so unobtrusively in a spittoon or in the bathroom. Kindly do not use ash-trays for this purpose.

In a nutshell, good manners and etiquette are based on those most endearing of qualities: kindness, thoughtfulness and consideration for others. We must stay sensitive to the feelings of others.

Chapter 29

GROOMING

"The apparel oft proclaimeth the Man."
— William Shakespeare

Make Appearance an Asset

Appearance is all important because it communicates something. The well-dressed person will add to his or her self-confidence and courage, and the careless and poorly dressed person will seldom make any great progress on the road to success. Always dress neatly and attractively. The consciousness of being well-dressed heightens one's self-respect and increases self-confidence. If a person has baggy trousers, unkempt shoes, ungroomed hair, fountain pen and pencils peeping out of his coat pocket, or a bulging, ugly handbag, the persons he transacts with are also likely to feel as little respect for him as he seems to feel for himself.

To act right, you have to look right and feel right. When you look good, you feel good and you act well. Therefore, always present a well-groomed, neat appearance. Always ensure that your appearance is neat, clean, tidy, well-dressed and appropriate. A well-groomed person gives the message to the world that he has high personal standards, efficiency and thoroughness. The ill-groomed person gives the opposite message. Your dress should always be appropriate for the occasion.

We have only 4 contacts with people. We are evaluated and classified by 4 things — by what we say, and how we say it, by what we do and by how we look.

Head to Foot Check-list

Men: -

a) **Hair:** should be well-combed and less oily. Neat and short hair is the best for an Executive look. It should also be well-styled; Avoid long side-burns; see that there is no hair on the forehead, ear and nose. If you are a turban-wearing Sikh, make sure that the turban is clean, starched and tied neatly.

b) **Face:** The clean-shaven look is always the best. It makes it look like you care about yourself. Advisable to use after-shave lotion. After-shave lotion should only be used as after-shave and should not be used in place of cologne /perfume.

   If bearded, ensure that beard is well-trimmed. It should be neat and not too long. It should not be unkempt or dishevelled. The same applies to Moustache. Eyes, Nose and Ears must be clean. You may go for facials - Facials are not for females only.

c) **Shirt**: Your shirt should be clean and well-pressed. Shirt should preferably be white or light colours; avoid fancy stuff; prints & silk. Stripes are acceptable, but they should not be big or large or bold stripes. Checks are also okay, but they should be subtle and small checks only. However, it is better to avoid stripes/ checks for formal occasions. Prefer solid colours, use Terry-cot shirts. Avoid polyester, Chinese silks, etc. Wear Anti-wrinkles shirt. Engage an excellent Tailor or buy better brands of ready-made shirts -

viz - Arrow, Allen Solly, Louis Philip, Zodiac, Van Heusen, etc. Although, half-sleeve shirt is now acceptable, it is advisable to wear full-sleeve shirts for formal occasions. The Collar of the shirt must be clean especially on neck-rim. Tips of collar must not be dog-eared. Cuffs must be clean and well-buttoned. Ensure that no buttons are missing.

d) **Trousers:** Trousers should be in Dark colours - Gray, Black, Brown, etc. They should be well-Tailored. Trousers should be worn high and be of proper length, i.e. coming up to shoes... For that, you must be in good shape. It is your responsibility to keep yourself fit and trim. It is difficult to be well-groomed if you are not fit, trim and in shape.

e) **Tie:** When wearing a Tie, shirt collar must always be Hard/stiff. Tie must be broad (not very broad) and well pressed. Tie should be up to the belt and match with Trousers. Never wash a Tie - Dry-clean it.

f) **Socks:** Preferably Dark and matching with Trousers/ shoes; socks should be of proper length and have good elastic to avoid any gap between socks and trousers. Avoid white socks.

g) **Shoes:** Use conservative shoes to match the suit/ trousers. Avoid sports/casual shoes. Avoid Moccasins; shoes should be practical, well-laced and well-polished. They should preferably be black, dark-brown or cherry.

h) **Hands:** Hands should always be clean, Nails should be short, well-cut and clean/manicured.

1) **General for Men:** Make sure your comb/handkerchief is not sticking out. Handkerchief should be clean, well-pressed, neatly folded and kept in the pocket of Trousers; Avoid awkward bulges in Trousers/Jackets. Don't carry big, heavy wallets in your Trousers/

Jackets. Don't carry Diaries/scraps of papers/heavy change, etc. in shirt pockets.

Women

a) **Hair:** Wear in a Bun. If not comfortable, hair should be left open, but it should be washed, combed and preferably styled. Hair should be brushed back neatly and tied properly.

b) **Face:** Ensure that there is no Facial hair; see that you have no hair on the upper lip. For women, waxing is essential. Being Hairy is not for women. Use light makeup. Wear lipstick - at least light - it will enhance your personality/your looks. Make-up should be applied to present a smooth facade and not to flaunt a vast and varied personal collection. Shades of lipstick and nail-enamel that border on the pale and unobtrusive, subdued eyes and a pleasant persona is what you must project.

c) **Dress:** Dress to make a subtle impact. Wear colours which suit you and enhance your looks. Introspect; find out what really suits you. Experiment till you hit the right combination.

d) **Blouses:** Blouses should be conservative, well-ironed and clean and should go well with the rest of the attire. For formal occasions, avoid wearing blouses which are too short and have plunging necklines, etc.

e) **Saree or Dress:** Saree must be of conservative colour. Printed sarees must be simple, well-pressed and well-draped. If you are not comfortable in a saree, you may wear Western or Indian formal dress. Silk sarees are the best. They should be sober/crepe silk. Avoid heavy silks. Avoid chiffon sarees because they are very transparent. Silks are more manageable. Sarees should be pleated and pinned-up for formal occasions.

The same applies to Dupattas. For social occa¬sions, however, you may leave them loose. They look more elegant.

Nowadays, salwar-kameez are acceptable for formal occasions. Nonetheless, it is advisable to avoid them for very formal occasions. Likewise, Business skirt/ blouse are also acceptable. So also are business Trousers. However, for formal occasions avoid Jeans/ Pants.

f) **Accessories:** Accessories should be kept to a bare minimum. Wear as few of them as possible. Chunky jewellery makes too much noise. Ear-rings; nose-rings, if any, should be conservative and small, i.e. no heavy, dangling, noise making jewellery. Avoid Big, Heavy stuff. Avoid Gold/silver.

g) **Hands:** Hands should be clean. Nails may be long, but they should be well-filed and well-manicured. If using nail-polish, see that the nails are well-painted. Nothing is more disagreeable than stained/ smudged/ mis-matched/chipped nail polish. Ensure that there are no broken nails. Go low on colours. Nail polish should be perfect; manicuring/filing are very important.

h) **Shoes:** shoes should be conservative and practical. They should be well-polished. High heels are the best. They add height to a woman and help a woman's gait/ walk. If not used to high heels, then it is ad¬visable to practice walking in them before wearing them on formal occasions. It is also preferable to wear closed shoes.

Feet should be well-pedicured and clean. If wearing western dress/skirt, black-stockings with shoes is a must.

i) **Perfume:** While choosing a perfume, again, subtlety is the rule. No hot stuff.

j) Voluminous bags and thick files make you appear tedious and dis¬organized. It is always best to carry as little as possible, thereby making sure that everything you need for the occasion is just a couple of seconds away. Also make sure that you don't hold kerchief in hand.

General

(1) Try to appear confident

(2) You need to look your best. Therefore, come what may, get a good night's sleep.

Some More Grooming Tips

1. Smile. It costs nothing. It is the Golden Rule.
2. Have a Firm Handshake.
3. Walk Erect. Have erect posture - stomach in / chest out; lean slightly forward; raise rib cage; no stoop; shoulder parallel to the ground; Feel the pull in the lower back.
4. Sitting: Sit back, Erect but not rigid; don't slouch; lean forward slightly to show interest/attention. Be professionally relaxed.
5. Mobiles should be off.
6. Body Language is very important. Have inner warmth. Give an image/ impression that you have "warmth".
7. Coming Across: How you come across, the total effect you create is most important. Speak well and ensure that you make a desirable impact.

Personal Hygiene: It is most important to use deodorant on your body at appropriate places, especially in Air—conditioned office. Deodorant is more important than cologne. Deodorant is not "feminine". Men should also use it. Don't spray Deodorant on your clothes. Use it on your skin. In a place like Mumbai because of its Humidity and travails of travel by local train, it may become necessary to use deodorant more often.

Chapter 30

VOICE CULTURE

Voice culture means bringing your voice under control. Voice is nothing but air which is forced through the vocal chords as you breathe out. The vibration creates a sound which we call voice. And that's your personality, your confidence. Your voice is you.

It is largely by means of words that we express different moods, attitudes, opinions or feelings. As speech has a vast range of precise symbols and grammar, it is the most indispensable of all means of self-expression. Humans can 'speak their mind'. But to portray the mind truly, the speech must have the correct voice. A fine mastery of words cannot reproduce the speaker's mind if the utterance is faulty, too soft, shrill or grates harshly upon the ear.

How do we, therefore, distinguish between a good and a bad voice. Well, very simply, learn to listen. Listen more if you wish to speak better. Good listening means creating a sensitive body, ear and mind because you listen not just with your ears, but with your entire being. Close your eyes and 'listen' to voices around you. Pick up the pleasant sounds. When you speak, sound pleasant.

Some ingredients of a winning voice (Do's)

- Divide your speech into thoughts and visuals.
- Speak from your stomach. It is the seat of all emotions

and breath.

- Converse and communicate. Do not merely pass on information.
- Energise your voice with correct breathing.
- Modulate your voice. Give it rhythm, texture, feelings and colour.
- Be real. Very real.
- Use the magic pause.

These are unacceptable! (Don't's)

- If you are inaudible and make the listener strain his ears.
- If you speak very fast without any pause.
- If you speak in one tone.
- If you are low on energy.
- If you produce a voice that is cold and unwelcome.
- If you project a voice that is artificial and put on.

Listen to your voice. Your voice reveals your level of energy. Keep it vibrant. Your voice is your personality, your confidence. Your Voice must make ears turn.

Voice is a culture that takes time to develop. Be patient. Make your voice energetic. It is very important to speak with energy and enthusiasm. Do not speak monotonously. A good voice will have the following characteristics:

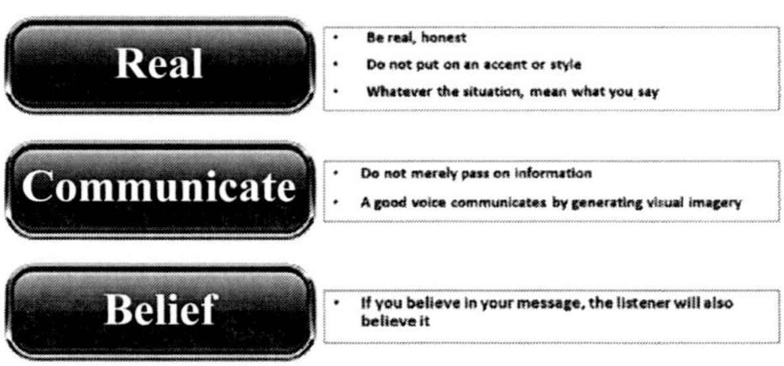

A few points to be kept in mind

- Enunciate: Pronounce words well. Enunciate clearly. Do not mumble.
- Variation: Have variation in your voice. Do not be flat, dull or monotonous. In order to do this:
  - Change your pitch
  - Increase/decrease volume
  - Vary speed of talking
  - Emphasize or stress words to convey the right meaning
  - Add colour to your voice. Mix the tone, pace, pauses, volume and pitch.
- Volume: Here are a couple of pointers:
  - Speak audibly. Be appropriately loud, but not too loud or too soft. Always be conscious of opening your mouth (do not open beyond a 3-finger distance).
  - Speak at correct speed, with effective pauses, before and after an important point or a major break in the thoughts, etc.
- Quality: Speak in a warm, pleasant tone. Do not speak in a distracting tone— too high, too nasal or too whining.
- Clarity: Be clear in your speech by using your organs of speech effectively. Voice is connected to your shoulders, neck, chest, back, spine and stomach.
- Emotions: This is very important. Identify with what you are talking. Feel joy and passion about your message or content.

Practical steps (exercises) to develop your voice

- Correct breathing is very important. Breathing has a direct effect on voice. You have to get your breathing right to get your articulation right. When we breathe shallow, we reduce our capacity to talk. Posture also determines how you speak. When you slouch, you reduce the capacity of your lungs. Do deep breathing exercises. Breath control means we consciously become aware of our breathing. Breathe in (inhale) for 5 counts. When you inhale, stomach comes out. Now, hold for 5 counts and then exhale for 5 counts. When you exhale, stomach comes in. Do this simple exercise for 5 minutes every morning and as frequently as possible throughout the day.
- It is important to remember that physical and mental fitness are very necessary. Unless you get into a fitness regime, your voice cannot improve. Talking requires a lot of physical fitness. Avoid oily stuff, aerated drinks, alcohol, smoking; do not overdo tea/ coffee, drink plenty of water. Eat honey. Also drink/ sip water during presentations. Avoid speaking on an empty stomach or when you are very tired.
- Read loudly for at least 10-15 minutes every day. Preferably read stuff which involves drama and dialogue.
- Do tongue exercises:
    - o Stick the tongue out as much as you can and then take the tongue in. Do this a few times daily. Also, roll your tongue around in the mouth.
    - o Say ‘a, b, c, d...y, z’ not by opening the mouth, but by stretching your mouth. You must feel pain in the cheeks if you do this exercise correctly.
    - o Say ‘urgent, detergent’ loudly and clearly a few times.
    - o Say ‘fud, dud, dud, da’ a few times. Vary the

volume and speed. Go high, go low, go fast, go slow.

The last four exercises will help to make your tongue and the mouth region flexible. This will help you to enunciate better.

- After the eyes, the most expressive part of one's face are the lips. Use them properly, be expressive. Exercise: say 'bit-bat, bit-bat' many times using only your lips and not opening your mouth. Keep varying the speed and volume.
- Practice saying tongue twisters a few times every day. Choose your own. A few examples are given here:
  - o Good blood, bad blood, bad blood, good blood
  - o Red leather, yellow leather, yellow leather, red leather
  - o Can cat-catchers catch caught cats
  - o She sells sea shells on the seashore
- To improve your articulation, pronounce words distinctly. Be fluent and clear in speech and clearly express an idea or feeling. Practice saying, as often as possible, the following four sentences:
  - o It is a very warm day.
  - o I love my son very much (replace with the name of the person dearest to you).
  - o These days, there is a lot of tension in Mumbai.
  - o I look forward to a sumptuous dinner.
- Do the following exercise to develop pause and variation. Say:

  Bright blue bubbles,

  Bobby blew and blew,

  Breathing, blowing, breathing,

  Behold...

Bobby became a bubble too.

- Adequate pause and emphasis help you to decorate your speech, i.e. to make it exciting. To acquire this, say the following verse a few times daily, with the right emphasis:

  My baby sister is really swell

  I love her smile

  But not her smell.

- For developing voice modulation, try to say the same words/sentences while expressing different emotions (such as happy, shy, angry, sad, jealous, sarcastic, suspicious). One practice phrase for you is "what's funny?" Try saying this using various emotions.
- Further, practice imitating different people — your friends, grandparents, the building watchman, a celebrity, etc.
- Repeat the following several times, with emphasis on a different word each time, as follows:
  - o This is my wife.
  - o This is my wife.
  - o This is my wife.
  - o This is my wife.

  You can easily see that the meaning of the sentence changes with the shift of emphasis.

- Projection of voice: There are four levels of pitch (throw/volume) — low, normal, high and very high. To acquire skills in projecting your voice correctly and moving adequately from one level to another, practice saying the following sentence quickly and changing the pitch from one level to another:

  'I will speak effectively and loudly.'

- For developing lung capacity, say the following in

one breath, one by one (easy to difficult) —add a new word at every step:

- I
- I can...
- I can control...
- I can control my...
- I can control my breath...
- I can control my breath and...
- I can control my breath and sustain...
- I can control my breath and sustain my...
- I can control my breath and sustain my phrasing.

Chapter 31

THE JOYS AND BENEFITS OF READING BOOKS

"Books are the carriers of civilization. Without books, history is silent, literature dumb, science crippled, thought and speculation at a standstill."

- Barbara Tuchman

A good book is the best friend of the wise. It is the most delightful companion a person can have. To develop a love for books, one needs to have a thirsty, curious and seeking mind.

Books widen your horizons. They open up vast vistas of knowledge, wisdom and inspiration. Books are a storehouse of information and wisdom. Books are the reservoirs of the noble thoughts and ideas of human beings through the ages. They expand your mind to encompass great ideas. They help to lift your sights and broaden your vision. Through books, you grow; you stretch your mind with the thoughts of great thinkers; you live many lives through books- you can discover America with Columbus, stand with Lincoln at Gettysburg, work in the laboratory with Edison and walk the fields with St. Francis or Gautam Buddha. In books, one can find an answer to every question, every problem that one faces. As Montesquieu said, "I have never known any trouble that an hour's reading did not assuage".

Walter Landor says, "What is reading, but silent conversation." A good conversation is almost an orgiastic experience. And in these techno-savvy days, when the art of conversation is dying, it is through books that you can be in a conversation with the noblest, greatest minds- a Lincoln, a Bertrand Russel, a Martin Luther King, an Einstein, etc. Through reading books, you can break free from the pettiness that may be surrounding you in your workplace, social circle or elsewhere and soar up in a rarefied atmosphere. In the words of Barbara Tuchman, "Books are humanity in prints."

Of course, there are books that are sheer junk and if you get into the habit of reading them, you will harm yourself because such books can poison your mind, make you biased and give you false values. Your mind is your garden. It is your responsibility to make your garden lush and beautiful. Therefore, be very selective about what you read. Plant the proper seeds into your mind and your mind will expand and grow. A mind once stretched by new ideas or information will never come back to its original, limited dimensions. Thus, what you read must be immensely nourishing, which will improve you and the quality of your life.

You can read fiction for relaxation, humour for entertainment and to bring

laughter in your life; autobiography or biography for inspiration, poetry for romance; self-development books for personal growth; philosophical and historical books to gain proper perspective; management books to learn managerial skills and leadership qualities; technical and professional books to upgrade your skills, etc. Treat-each book according to its merit. As someone wisely said, "Some books are meant to be tasted, some are meant to be chewed and, finally, some books are meant to be digested fully."

A book worth reading is a book worth buying [John Ruskin]. Read with concentration and always read with a pen or pencil in your hand. Underline the words, ideas, passages that appeal to you the most so that you can quickly review the heart of the book. A great book should be read many times- at least ten to fifteen times. To get the best out of a great book, you must study it minutely like what you would do with important documents. Ponder over what you read; reflect over it and let its wisdom or message engulf you and become your own.

Read something each day. Discipline yourself to a regular schedule of reading. Feed your mind constantly. Don't just feed your body. Feeding your mind is as important, if not more important than, feeding your body. One lover of books put it beautifully when he said "When I have some money, I buy books. If any money is left, then I buy food." Reading for 30 minutes a day will do wonders for you-----it will make a delightful difference to your life. A person who knows but does not read is like a person who has not learnt to read at all.

Develop the skill to read several books at a time, turning from one to another as your moods or desire or energy levels change---a novel, a biography, a self-improvement book, a volume of history, a professional book, a work of science, etc.

Read to increase your knowledge, your background, your awareness, and your insight. Read to grow-----read to lead-remember readers are leaders and leaders are readers.

Some may argue that what you get through a book can easily be obtained through the Internet. That may be true. But a book is personal, a book is warm, a book is almost human. It can be caressed, it can be fondled. And, as Daniel J. Boorstin says, "A wonderful thing about a book in contrast to a computer screen, is that you can take a book to bed with you."

Chapter 32

THE LAW OF ATTRACTION

Everything in the universe is made up of energy. Every object in the universe has got a frequency. Whatever object you want to attract in life you have to send the frequency of that object and you will receive it. We human beings send our frequency to the universe through our thoughts, words and actions.

Example of thinking: - A man and his wife are staying in a one BHK house. The man thinks that they are only 2 persons in the house and the house is big enough for them. He is sending the frequency of one BHK House.

Example of words: - A husband and wife are discussing with each other how the recession is negatively affecting their finances and how they will never become rich. Thus, they are sending the frequency of "being poor" or "not being rich'.

Example of action: - A man is not happy with his job. He wants a change. But he does not search for one or go for interviews. He is sending the frequency of "being stuck" in his present job.

The process outlined above is akin to the working of a mobile phone. Every mobile number has got a sim card and every sim card has got a frequency. Whenever we dial a mobile number, that ten-digit number has a frequency which matches with the frequency of that sim card, so after dialling that number it gets connected to that number.

The Law of Attraction (LOA) states that "like attracts like" and "whatever we focus on expands". It takes this concept to a deeper level; the level of thought. According to this Law, we attract circumstances, material objects and people to us according to the thoughts we consistently hold in mind. Our thinking creates and brings to us whatever we think about. It applies to everyone, in every situation, at all times, whether you realize it or not - without exception. You get what you think about, good or bad.

How does LOA Work? We need to tune our thoughts, words, actions. Tuning our thoughts, words, actions towards our goal begins to attract the people and circumstances necessary to accomplish the goal. It's not that resources never existed before. It's just that our mind never focused on finding them.

Your focus, your Attention (your Dominant thought) must be on "what you desire" and not the opposite, i.e. not on "what you don't desire". Often, even when you believe you are thinking about something that you desire, you are actually thinking about the exact opposite of what you desire. In other words, when you make statements like, for e.g. "I want to be well: I don't want to be sick" or " I want to have financial security, I don't want to experience a shortage of money" or " I want the perfect relationship to come to me: I don't want to be alone". Your attention, your focus is on "what you don't want rather than on what you want".

What you think and what you get is always a perfect vibrational match. Focus on what you want because what you focus on expands in your life. Your attention must be on it (on what you want) and not on the lack of it. Source Energy receives your vibrational request and, by the Law of Attraction, offers an immediate response.

As long as you are more aware of what you do not want regarding a situation, what you do want cannot come to you.

For e.g. your car is getting older and is beginning to require frequent repairs. As you begin to notice its fading beauty, you find yourself desiring a new car. But instead of immediately turning your attention towards your fresh new desire, you look back at the vehicle you currently own, pointing out the reasons why you desire the new car. "This old car no longer pleases me" you conclude not realizing that in looking at the unpleasant car, you are taking your vibration back to it, and not forward to the new car you desire. "I really need a new car" you explain, pointing out the dents, the cracks and the undependable performance of the old one. With each statement of need and justification for a new car, you unwittingly reinforce the vibration of your current, unpleasant situation, and in doing so, you continue to hold yourself out of vibrational alignment with your new car and out of the receiving mode of what you are asking for.

As long as you are more aware of what you do not want regarding this situation, what you do want cannot come to you. In other words, if you are predominantly thinking about your beautiful new car, then it is steadily making its way to you, but if you are predominantly thinking about your undependable current car, your dependable new car cannot move towards you.

The Law of Attraction says: "That which is like unto itself is drawn." And so, the essence of whatever you give your attention to is unfolding in your experience. Therefore, there is nothing that you cannot be, do or have. That is the Law.

If there is something you desire that you currently do not have, you need only put your attention upon it and by the Law of Attraction, it will come to you. And, if there is something that you desire that you currently do not have, and you put your attention on your current state of "not having it', then Law of Attraction, will continue to match the "not having it" vibration, so that you will continue to "not have" that which you desire. It is the Law. The key to bringing something into your experience that you desire is to achieve vibrational harmony with what you desire.

You get what you predominantly think about, whether you want it or not. Whatever you experience in Life, you have invited every bit of it through your own thought process. Nothing can occur in your life experience without your invitation to it through your thought. There are no exceptions to the powerful Law of Attraction and you get what you think about. By the powerful Universal Law of Attraction, you draw to you the essence of whatever you are predominantly thinking about. So, if you are predominantly thinking about the things that you desire, your Life experiences reflect those things. And in the same way if you are predominantly thinking of what you don't want, your life experience reflects those things.

STEPS TO ATTRACT THINGS THRU LAW OF ATTRACTION

1. Goal: - Our goal must be very clear and specific as to what we want. The goal has to be in writing. If it is not on paper, then it may keep on changing. For example, today you desire to have, say, a Maruti - Wagon R and after a few days you decide you like Scorpio and after a fortnight you start thinking about Honda City. In such a situation you send mixed frequency and mixed frequency will not give you mixed results, but it will give you no result. That is why the goal has to be in writing so that we don't change it.

2. Emotions: Whatever goal you have set you should associate a lot of positive emotions with it. This means it should mean a lot to you and you should be very excited and interested in having that thing in your life. If you want something but you associate negative emotions with that you will not attract it. For example, your goal is to become very wealthy, but you feel that money is the root of all evil or money will make you less spiritual and bring in worries and misery in your life. In this case you will not attract wealth because you have associated negative emotions with money. So, whatever you desire, you should actually feel that it is the best thing in your life and all your thoughts about that thing should be positive.

3. Belief: Whatever you have selected as your goal and after you have added a lot of positive emotions to it you have to believe that it is yours. You have to believe that it is in the process of reaching you and you should not have the slightest doubt about it. Belief is the most important ingredient in the entire law of attraction process.

4. Affirmation: (Affirmation is the subject matter of a separate chapter). Affirmation is repeating the positive statement in the present continuous tense. Affirmation is a tool which changes our negative thoughts and adds positive emotions to our thoughts. Affirmation can be done in 3 ways; counter; recording; writing.

5. Visualization: (This has been dealt with in a separate chapter); Visualization is the process of creating, in a totally relaxed state, mental images of the things you want. In this process you actually enjoy the object you want. Throughout the process (about 20 minutes) of visualization you should feel that the object is yours and you have to create the same feeling of happiness that you will have when you actually get the object. Ideally, visualization should be done just before you go .to sleep at night and the first thing as soon as you wake up in the morning.

6. Gratitude: Gratitude is the process wherein you keep on thanking the universe throughout the day for all the good things happening in your life. Every time you express gratitude, every time you appreciate something, every time you praise something, every time you feel good about something, you are telling the universe; “More of this, please.’ In other words, ‘if you are mostly in a state of appreciation and gratitude, all good things will flow to you. The more you appreciate what you have right now, the more things will flow into your life!

7. Action: It is crucial that you take appropriate action to get what you want. Figure out all the different ways that you can move towards what you want to achieve and act promptly. The last few letters of the word "Attraction" are "action".

We may end by saying that the law of attraction always works perfectly when you align every part of your mind, body and action with each other.

Chapter 33

BE UPSET FREE - DECONDITION YOUR MIND

MAN IS THE ONLY ANIMAL WHO CAN CHANGE OVERNIGHT

Man is a bundle of habits. These habits may be hygienic, productive, self – fulfilling, etc. or, on the other hand, they may be unhygienic, counterproductive, self-destroying, etc. In other words, habits may be good habits or bad habits. First, we make our habits, then the habits make us and shape our responses, thoughts, actions.

We observe that the same event leads different people to feel different emotions. Supposing I am talking to my friend and suddenly a dog appears near us. Since I am afraid of dogs and uncomfortable with them, I will feel fear, anxiety, worry and take immediate action to move away from the scene. On the other hand, my friend who is a lover of dogs and is very comfortable with them will feel delighted & happy and start petting the dog & talking to the dog. Thus, the event is the same, but the consequences are different.

Simple events like receiving a gruff reply, reading a newspaper, watching a movie lead to different emotions ranging from plain irritation to happiness to guilt and revenge. The same event leads different people to feel different emotions.

Thus, an event may not be in my hand but the stimulus, the response certainly is. In other words, I am free to choose my emotions. I am not a puppet in the hands of others. External events cannot compel me to have any particular emotions.

The external world "triggers". It is the activating event - the activating event A leads to consequences (C). C is of two types - internal (fear, anxiety, worry) and external (behaviour, running away from the dog for e.g.). My behaviour is the result of my emotion; my emotion is the result of my thinking (as you think, so you feel).

Between A and C is 'B' (my self - talk in which I indulge every minute). 'B' is my "belief', my "Baggage", - my "Baloon" which is made up of my ideas, attitudes, aspirations, past experiences, ambitions, dreams, goals, etc. Simply put, we all carry in our heads what Anthony D'mello calls a "model of reality'. This model has been created by the "programming" we received, the "indoctrination" imposed on us; the "conditioning" we were subjected to, the customs, the traditions, the trainings, the education, the experiences, etc which were provided to us. When the behaviour of persons around us and the events of life are in consonance with or conform to the model we have created, we are happy and at peace, but when they are at variance to our model, we feel annoyed, uncomfortable. We are "upset". Thus, what really upsets us is not the events or the persons but the model, the Baggage that we carry in our head.

The French Philosopher Montaigne said, "A man is not hurt by what happens but is hurt by his opinion of it". Confucius said, "A man is robbed only if he thinks of it". Being robbed or wronged is nothing, if you don't remember it. Thus, I have the freedom to choose my own emotions.

My upset does not come from outside reality, but from my inner conditioning. If I remove the 'conditioning, if I change my 'beliefs' my upset disappears. The 'model' that I have created in my mind is the result of many "accidental" factors

- the family I was born in; the school I went to; the social framework in which I operated; the environment in which I thrived, etc. This "model" is arbitrary and accidental. When you realize that, you will not feel upset anymore at anything.

Something that upsets you may not upset another person. It shows that the upset is caused not by any objective reality but by your own perception of it. The model, the Belief, the Baggage, the Programming; the conditioning in your head is different from the model in the other person's mind and so you are affected by the incident while the other is not. Valles pointedly gives this example and I quote; "A married man in India would be upset if he invited a guest to his house and the guest would sleep with his (the Host's) wife. An Eskimo, apparently, is not upset if his guest behaves in that way, and may in fact, invite him to do so. The two married men have different mental models of what is proper, and so react differently. The outside fact is the same, but the inner perception differs. Change your perception and you will change your reaction. The point of the example is that you must not blame your inner upset on outside causes. It comes from inside. From your conditioned brain."

It is said that life is empty and meaningless. The only meaning it has is the meaning we give to it. Thus, in most parts of the world, a diamond is regarded as very precious, but it is seen as valueless by some African tribes. Likewise, children love and enjoy playing in the dirt while we, adults, recoil at it. It all depends on the model, the conditioning, the programming, the picture created in the brain. It is abundantly clear from the above that only physical pain is real. All other sufferings- mental, emotional, psychological - is created by my inner programming and does not come from objective causes. Thus, I have to only change the inner programme and the upset will cease. Simply put, as the Bard said. "Nothing is good or bad but thinking makes it so".

Nobody upsets you, you upset yourself. Don't give anyone

permission to annoy you, to upset you, to get on your nerves. Don't surrender to another person the power over life. Don't make yourself a helpless victim. Remember that any suffering in your life, except physical pain, comes from yourself, from within. Shoulder the responsibility for your suffering.

My programming, my brainwashing, my conditioning has created a prefabricated structure which dictates how I feel and act. I am a slave to my conditioning which forces me now to feel good in certain situations and bad in others in a wholly arbitrary way. I need to free myself, to reclaim my power over my life. My conditioning has created a lot of illusions in my mind - the illusion that I need money to be happy; the illusion that I need this person or this thing or this result or this circumstance, etc., to be happy and fulfilled. All these are illusions created in the mind by indoctrination and well-meant brainwashing. The action point is to drop these illusions one by one and realize for yourself that nothing is really necessary to be upset free and happy. Keep clearing your brain from all the clutter, dirt and rust that it has gathered and accumulated over the years and be upset free and happy and healthy.

Chapter 34

BE A GIVER (Practice the Law of Giving)

"Give and it will be given to you... for the measure you will give will be the measure you get back"

- *Luke 6.38*

"Happiness and success both depend on your ability to give. This ability is in your consciousness, in your mind. And it is not the object that you give that matters, but the attitude of sharing."

- *Sri Sri Ravishankar*

"You will not attain piety until you expend what you love, and whatever thing you expend, God knows of it."

- *Quran 3.92*

The above quotations bring out, very forcefully, the importance of the Law of Giving. In his book, 'The Seven Spiritual Laws of Success', Deepak Chopra has included the Law of Giving as one of the seven laws.

Giving is a beautiful experience. By practicing giving, you make a difference to others and yourself. It is a powerful feeling to be able to give regularly. By giving, you can live to your potential, avoid loneliness, become fearless, touch your spirit and find meaning and fulfilment. The universe is abundant. As Azim Jamal says, "The more you are in the flow of giving, the more abundance flows through you."

According to Deepak Chopra, practicing the Law of Giving is very simple: if you want joy, give joy to others. If you want love, learn to give love. If you want attention and appreciation, learn to give attention and appreciation. If you want material affluence, help others to become materially affluent. In fact, the easiest way to get what you want is to help others get what they want. In the same vein, Zig Ziglar says, "You can get anything you want in life provided you help enough other people to get what they want."

And RW Emerson asserts that "It is one of the beautiful compensations of this life that no one can sincerely try to help another without helping himself."

According to Skip Ross, the first principle on which the Law of Giving is based is "Give and you receive." This principle is expressed in different ways: 'The law of action and reaction', 'the law of radiation and attraction', 'the law of cause and effect', 'the law of sowing and reaping', etc. What you plant is what you get — if you plant corn, you get corn. If you plant love, you get love. Whatever you give is what you receive.

You may say that you do not have enough for yourself, so how can you give to others?

The second principle answers this. It says, "You always have something to give." Everyone can give something. Even if you cannot give money or material objects, you can give a smile, praise, encouragement, attention, caring, love, wisdom, skills, leadership, advice, hope, laughter, respect, etc. You can give the simple gift of touch. Touch is a gift that everyone can give. Physical touch is a basic human need. One of the best gifts that you can give is your respect, displayed through active listening. You can give a word of praise. We are built up by praise and destroyed by criticism. If you give praise, you will receive praise that builds you up. When you give criticism, you are in the process of destroying yourself. You can show respect to all people, regardless of their social status, gender, age or religion. When you give wholeheartedly and with good intentions, you set in motion a powerful force. The day you are able to feel joy in giving no matter what your status, is the day you find bliss in life.

Giving enriches your life with meaning, fulfilment and happiness. It liberates you to unlock your potential and create breakthroughs. It is a privilege, an honour, to give. Therefore, give freely and generously of your time, knowledge, wisdom, wealth, love, etc. and experience the power and beauty of giving. Giving creates a symbiotic relationship. It benefits both parties. The receiver benefits from your gift. And you benefit personally by virtue of having been a giver. Giving brings meaning to your life. And remember that giving possessions, wealth, material objects, is good, but real giving is giving of yourself and that has more impact.

The third principle of giving is that you give and give, over and over again, not knowing when it will come back to you or how, but expecting that ultimately, you will receive. Your rewards may be instantaneous, or they may take a while, but giving always has rewards. And when the rewards come, be open to receiving them, for giving and receiving are the two sides of the same coin.

The principles of giving work powerfully in every area of life. According to Skip Ross, the principle of giving begins to develop a storehouse from which we give in greater abundance. As we give, in return, we receive more, which increases the storehouse from which we give. He says that "it is possible to give away and become richer! It is also possible to hold on too tightly and lose everything. Yes, the liberal man shall be rich. By watering others, he waters himself.

The benefits of giving

- By giving, you unlock your potential.
- You become fearless.
- You avoid or overcome loneliness.
- You find meaning and fulfilment in your life.
- The more you are in the flow of giving, the more abundance flows through you.
- Giving helps to develop new relationships.
- Giving builds a feeling of security in the mind of the giver.
- It results in good health, happiness, peace and love.
- The giver develops a sense of accomplishment, empowerment and pride.
- Giving reduces self-centeredness.
- An important form of giving is doing volunteer work in society. Doing volunteer work selflessly has immense benefits. It enhances your immune system, lowers cholesterol levels, strengthens your heart, decreases the incidence of chest pains and generally reduces stress.

Finally, always remember that when you help others to meet their needs, you increase the likelihood of meeting your own needs.

Moral reasons for giving

No man is an island by himself. No human being is completely independent.' We are all inter-dependent. We were born as a result of the physical activity of two persons and from the time of our conception, during the course of our life, we have received many things from other people — our parents, elders, teachers, siblings, relatives, neighbours, strangers, etc. The schools we attended, the hospitals that took care of us, the cars/buses/trains we travel in, were all conceived and built by the hard work and money of other human beings. In fact, virtually everything we use in our life has been made by someone else. And it behoves us to give back to the universe, to society from whom we have received so much and continue to receive so much more.

It is apt to point out that all religions advocate/promote generosity. For example, Christianity encourages and emphasizes charity (the concept of 'tithing — giving 10% of your income to charity). Islam exhorts its followers to help others and give to people in need (the institution of 'zakat', whereby 2.5% of a Muslim's total worth has to be given to the poor and the needy). Likewise, in Judaism, 'tzedakah' or charity is the prescription to build a better world and in Hinduism, generosity is lauded and perceived as a possible path to salvation. We may conclude that if only everyone gave a little more, our world would be a more just, more peaceful, a healthier and happier place.

Giving up habits

Giving includes giving up harmful habits and practices. We are creatures of habits. First, we make our habits and then our habits make us, and sometimes un-make us, for habits can be productive or unproductive. We should, therefore, work towards giving up our bad or unproductive habits such as excessive sleeping, excessive television watching, unrestrained smoking, using drugs, drinking heavily, procrastinating, etc. These habits are big obstacles to our progress and seriously dampen our ability to give. If you give up these bad habits, you will free time to improve yourself, to develop yourself, to become a better, healthier and wiser person and to enhance your personal growth and your ability to give to others.

In addition, you must also give up or drop some bad, unproductive mental habits such as:

- Worrying about the future
- Holding limiting beliefs
- Trying to please everyone
- Saying 'yes' all the time, especially when you want to say 'no'
- Feeling sorry for yourself
- Holding or clinging to the past
- Not getting rid of negative people around you

We may conclude this chapter by saying that giving is a very beautiful experience. You can make a difference to yourself and to others if you practice giving regularly. Giving is empowering. It is liberating.

Make a decision that anytime you come in contact with anyone, you will give them something — not necessarily something material — it can be a flower, a compliment, a radiant smile, a blessing, etc.

Make a decision to give wherever you go, to whomsoever you meet; the more you give, the more confidence you will gain in the miraculous effects of this law. And as you receive more, your ability to give more will also increase.

Chapter 35

LIVE IN THE PRESENT

I had spent a lot of time and energy in my younger days to find an answer to the question "Why are we here?" It was futile. I realized that it was not possible, at least for me, to find the ultimate answer to this existential question. I became humble and started asking myself a more modest question viz. "Am I really here"? "Am I always where I really am?" Reflecting intensely on this, I was pained to realize that most of the time I just was not where I was.

I realized that the only moment that we really have is the present moment. And yet we do not live the present moment fully. We sully the present moment with distractions. We plague ourselves with thoughts of yesterday and tomorrow. We never fully do what we are actually doing. We do not give it our full attention. We mix up things. We talk when we eat. We watch TV while we are talking on the phone. We shake hands with one person while looking at or even talking to another. We are experts at being where we are not, when eating ice-cream, for e.g. we are worrying / thinking about myriad things and we consume the ice-cream mechanically without really fully savouring and enjoying it. When we are in the office, we worry about the domestic problems at home and when we are at home, we worry about the unfinished work in the office. When we are with the special friend, we are thinking about the spouse and when we are with the spouse, we are worrying about the friend. I am willing to wager that at this moment whilst reading this sentence, the reader is thinking of something else-maybe about his dinner or about an argument with a colleague/boss/child, etc.

A Latin precept says "Age quod agis", i.e., "Do what you do" This means that whatever you happen to do at the present moment, do it with your entire being. In other words, don't be distracted. Be completely with what you are doing. As Gautam Buddha once said: "Walk when you walk; talk when you talk; eat when you eat." Unfortunately, most of us are always "distracted" — while doing one thing, we are thinking of other things. That is why so often when we are commuting or working in the office, we are, struck by a thought "Did I put the geyser off? Did I lock the house door properly? This tendency also causes simple, avoidable mistakes in the letters and reports that we write. All this happens because while doing those things, we had failed to give those activities our full attention. We had failed to live in the moment.

The literal meaning of the word "Distract" is to tear apart. So, when we are distracted, we virtually tear ourselves to shreds, we are not whole, and we are not one, we are divided. And as Lincoln observed "A House divided against itself cannot stand." When we are not fully in the present, we allow our mental screen to be flooded with images of yesterday's failures/incidents and/or we project on our screen tomorrow's concerns and fears. In either case, we do not live fully in the here and now which is the only real moment we have. As Will Rogers said, "We allow tomorrow to eat up too much of our today." Oftentimes, during a discussion or a meeting or an Interview, I do not come up with the right response because my mind is cluttered with "distractions" and then the next day, when it is too late, I come up with the right answer, the right response and I torture myself endlessly because it did not come up when it should have.

This does not mean that yesterday and tomorrow, the past and the future have no relevance or significance. Of course, they have meaning. We must learn from the past and plan for the future, but we must not forget to live in the present. We must care and provide for the future. Whatever practical action we take in the present moment with the hope of securing our future is living in the present for e.g. buying Insurance policy; booking rail/air tickets in advance; students preparing for forthcoming examinations /Interviews; financial planning for retirement, etc. All this is perfectly fine and desirable. Nothing wrong with it. The problem arises when we cram our mind with thoughts about the past and the Future; when we overload our minds with concerns and worries; when we clutter our minds with memories, fears, worries, regrets, etc. and miss the beauty of the present moment. We miss the present by reminiscing nostalgically about the past and fearing and worrying about the future. This “Excess baggage” also reduces our effectiveness to deal with the present moment and the situation at hand. It undermines our vitality and destroys our spontaneity. The best preparation for the future is the proper use of the present.

When it comes to people, we tend to take them for granted. We do not relate to them with fresh eyes. We put stamps and labels on people. We form images of a person and then cease to relate to the person and instead relate to the image that we have formed of that person. A person is not the same always. He keeps on changing. He grows, He evolves. Heraclitus said: “You cannot enter the same river twice”. It is flowing; it is new every moment. So is a human being. He is fluid. He is constantly changing. We must learn to observe people, to take stock of people afresh and then relate to them. George Bernard Shaw once said: “My tailor is the wisest of all the persons who come to see me. Every time he comes, he takes new measurements.” Barry Stephens said: “Every time we meet is the first time.” This is because we change constantly.

Unfortunately, we not only label persons but we also classify and label groups, communities and nationalities for e.g. “All Indians are “; “All Muslims are….”, “All Women are…..”; “All Sports person are….”; “All Politicians are…”, etc. And this tendency leads to unhappy and disastrous consequences.

One way in which we spoil the present is that we build up expectations and we indulge in comparisons for e.g. while watching Shah Rukh Khan performing in “Devdas” or “Don” we tend to compare him with Dilip Kumar and Amitabh Bachchan in the same role respectively. In other words, we are not enjoying the present moment fully. Likewise, while watching a film, we tend to compare it with the book we have already read, or we approach an author’s second book, with great expectation because his first was a classic and then we are disappointed. When we see a good scenery, we immediately compare it with the beautiful scenery we enjoyed in the past or if we receive flowers now, we immediately tend to compare and reminisce about flowers we received in the past. In all such cases we do not savour the present moment fully. And often as Carlos G Valles says, “The comparison with the best lessens the enjoyment of the good and the comparison with the past lessens the enjoyment of the present.”

An offshoot of the habit of comparison is that it gives rise to envy. Then, as Bertrand Russel said, “Instead of deriving joy and happiness from what we have, we derive pain from what others have”. Carlos G Valles narrates the case of a woman who was married to a splendid man but who nevertheless was unhappy because her sister was married to a better man. In the words of C.G.Valles, “When we are not living in the present, we lose contact with reality” and “Not living in the present is refusal to accept reality”.

When we are in our “Circle of concern” we only grumble and criticize. We have no responsibility for any action. But when we are in our “Circle of Influence” we can change things. We can shoulder responsibility and take action. Living in the present also means being in your “Circle of Influence”.

Thus, 'Living' in the present means feeling joy and fulfilment now, in the present moment in whatever you happen to be doing and not waiting for something to happen like getting a promotion or having more money before you start enjoying life. We miserably fail to enjoy the present moment. We keep on postponing living. We are so good at living for tomorrow that we forget to live today. This approach is very truly and sadly reflected in the following lamentation: -

"First I was dying to finish School and start College
Then I was dying to finish College and start working
Then I was dying to marry and have children
Then I was dying for Children to grow old enough
for school so I could return to work
Then I was dying to retire from work
And now, I am really dying.......and
suddenly I realize that I forgot to "LIVE"
It would be profitable to remember that: -
Yesterday is History,
Tomorrow is a Mystery,
Today is a Gift, That's why
It is called The Present

ENJOY THIS GIFT. DON'T LOSE IT. DON'T WASTE IT.
Live life fully in the present.

Chapter 36

LET GO & GROW

(*The content in this chapter is influenced by the Book "Letting Go. Uncomplicating your Life" by Ramona Shepherd Adams, Herbert A Otto and Au Deane Shepherd Cowley*)

We clutter our lives with unnecessary things. We allow too many pressures, responsibilities, demands, expectations, material possessions, etc. to overwhelm our lives. One of the first steps to achieve personal growth is to un-complicate our lives — to Simplify. As Thoreau said: "Simplify, Simplify. Instead of 3 meals a day, if it be necessary eat but one; instead of a hundred duties, five and reduce other things in proportion." Thus, we must learn to let go of these clutters which fragment our lives. Letting go is a very important and critical skill to enhance personal growth and become an authentic person. A few of the areas in which we need to practice 'Letting Go' are:

a) **"Material Possessions":** We fill our lives with a plethora of useless and unwanted things. These things are unused and unappreciated. Our cupboards and lofts are full of goods and things we don't need or have time to enjoy. These possessions often only add to our load of worries and concerns. They become energy blocks which hamper personal growth. We need to ruthlessly remove them from our lives.

b) **"Outside Pressures":** We allow our lives to get

cluttered by manifold outside pressures and demands. They erode our peace of mind. There are pressures of work [Often we work late and sometimes we take work home too]; demands from Spouse/Children, acquaintances, Friends, Neighbours and Relatives, Societal and Community demands; demands to attend meetings, weddings, parties, funeral services, etc. There is always a demand to "Do" something and there is no time to just "Be". We often forget that we are "Human Beings" and not "Human Doings". We succumb to such pressures because we want to look "Good" in the eyes of other people. We need to let go of our need to feel wanted, appreciated and admired by others. In order to outgrow this need, we need to develop an attitude which says: "What others think of me is none of my business". In short, we need to learn to say "Yes" to very little and learn to say "No" to demands and pressures from social obligations, relatives, friends, family. We need to "Create" some time for ourselves which is exclusively our own and which we can use for personal growth, for doing things which give us most happiness, and that which relax, rejuvenate and regenerate us.

c) **"Worn-Out/Tired Relationships":** We hold on to relationships which have little meaning left for us. We need to accept the fact that people do outgrow each other. In relationships which are devitalized, the old spark goes, and persons involved become a drag on each other. It would be refreshing to let go of such relationships. Another type of tired relationships is Dead Relationships for e.g. former spouses/lovers/ mentors, etc. You can regain your freedom, get on with life and grow by letting go of these relationships. "Possessive relationships are found in Man/Woman, Parent/Child relationships. Here people behave as if they "Own" the other. Letting go of such relationships will enable one to regain her self-worth, self-reliance, authenticity and bring about a new energy and vitality in one's life.

d) **"Old Labels":** We tend to "Define" ourselves, to put "Labels" on ourselves. For e.g. "That is the way I am, I cannot help it", "I'm short-tempered, that's my nature". By labelling ourselves thus, we become rigid and predictable. Our words have a powerful impact on our personalities. They become a self-fulfilling prophesy and we end up becoming our labels. Labels thus are a huge obstacle to growth. We need to let go of such labels which limit us.

e) **"Clinging to the Past":** Many of us are stuck in the past and keep thinking and talking about how things used to be. We reminisce and are, often full of regrets and remorse. Our past becomes a heavy, unproductive burden. Life is a dynamic process and we need to learn to respond fully and energetically to the present. We have to learn to let go of past events, behaviours and ideas which were relevant and meaningful at one time but have now become excess baggage.

f) **"Useless Traditions & Practices":** We clutter our lives with "Shoulds" and "Oughts" that are absolutely irrelevant and meaningless to our present reality. Many of our Traditions and Practices got started and supported for irrational reasons. We need to examine them and preserve only those which are useful and add meaning, lustre and joy to our lives and let go of all those which have become excess baggage and only weigh us down.

g) **"Security Blankets":** A "Security Blanket" is an excessive, unreasonable need that must be present for a person to feel secure, valued and important. Some examples of such blankets are money, material possessions, family name, parent's achievements, Spouse's position, children's success and recognition, influential friends, and relatives, Guruji's eminence, club and professional memberships. If the security blanket is taken away, the person is devastated and feels worthless and lost. We need to let go of these blankets because they are external sources of security and can be snatched away by other persons or events. The only real security we have is our own inner assurance and strength.

h) **"Unhealthy Habits":** Man is a creature of Habits. We first make our habits and then our habits make us. Our habits can be productive and life-enhancing or they can be constrictive and life-destroying. Some of the common constrictive habits are: Over-eating; Smoking; excessive alcohol consumption; doing drugs; talking too much; worrying endlessly; watching TV excessively; excessive sleeping, etc. We need to let go of our destructive habits because they impede personal growth and, in their place plant good constructive habits which will result in personal growth and development.

A friend once told Emerson that "The World is coming to an end tonight". Emerson replied "That does not bother me. I can get along without it". That is the essence of the message of "Let Go": The only way to enjoy something fully in life is to be able to part with it; to be able to let it go.

Chapter 37

STAND TALL, BE COUNTED AND MAKE A MARK

Mother Teresa once said that we all are not expected to do "Extra Ordinary things", we are only expected to do ordinary things in an "Extra Ordinary" manner. Shiv Khera says, "Winners do not do different things, they do things differently."

Some people have huge talents and make a mark for themselves in this world in their chosen fields. The rest of us settle for mediocrity, for being "average". By this, we tell the world that we are only a face in the crowd. We don't count for anything. You can lead an ordinary life but by doing certain things you can stand out from the crowd, you can be a cut above the rest—certain things which are easy to do and because they are easy to do they are also easy not to do.

To stand out from the crowd do the following: -

- **Be a person of total reliability and integrity:** Always keep your word even in very small things. Be true to your word; fulfil your commitments even in small things like making or returning a telephone call if you have promised to do so; being punctual and always arriving on time; lending a book when you have promised to do so. A person of excellence goes the extra mile to do what is right. Keep your word even when it's difficult. If you do not value your words, no one else will. Always act on principles and not on expediency. Do what is right and not what is expedient. Once you establish a reputation for being reliable and a person of integrity, you will stand tall and be counted.

- **Apply the 4-way test:** When you are talking about someone to somebody else or when somebody is talking to you about somebody else apply the 4-Way test, i.e.

  1. Is the information about to be revealed completely true?
  2. Are we saying good or positive things about somebody?
  3. Is it kind to say it?
  4. Is it absolutely necessary to say it?

  If the answer to any of the above is "No", refuse, absolutely refuse, to say or listen to it.

- **Never ever talk ill behind people's back** and if you are in a group of people who are back-biting and bad-mouthing someone who is not present, make it a point to defend the person who is absent even if that makes you unpopular with those who are present and are doing the back-biting. In the course of time, your loyalty to the absent friend will convince the others that you will be loyal to them also if and when the time comes.

- **Treating People with Courtesy:** Another way to stand out from the crowd is to always treat people with courtesy and respect. Small acts like opening doors for people; letting people come out of the lift before you enter; always using courtesy words like "Please", "Thank you". will enhance your personality. In particular, always treat people below you in rank and position with utmost courtesy and respect for the true test of a person's character is how he treats a person who, he thinks, cannot harm him or help him.

- **Avoid Profanity:** In these days of permissiveness, it has become fashionable to be profane in the use of language. Using uncontrolled profanity is not only "Boorish and Offensive" but also betrays the lack of class and neither adds beauty nor strength to your communication. An occasional expletive may be appropriate but, by and large, a man of class will communicate effectively without using profanity. If you exercise control on your language, especially in volatile & explosive situations, you will stand out from the crowd.
- **Be Sensitive to Your Social Responsibilities:** You can show your class by being conscious of and taking pains to do certain activities in a correct manner for e.g. not parking in no parking areas; not parking at a spot reserved for handicapped persons; not honking in "Silence Zone", doing certain small things like taking good care of others' property for e.g. not wasting electricity or stationery at your workplace and mundane things like not leaving hotel rooms with lights on, the air-conditioners going full blast & T.V blaring. Likewise, while at a Mall or Departmental store, taking extra care and pains to replace books/ cereals/clothes, etc. in their proper places.
- **Integrity in Speech:** A person of integrity always says what he means and means what he says. When speaking, always speak the truth, nay the whole truth. If what you speak is true, but you don't state all the relevant facts, then you can deliberately confuse and mislead people. In relating events, stick to facts- don't give a slant or twist. This one quality alone will show that you are streets ahead of most people, you stand out and that you are in a class of your own; a cut above

the rest.

- **Money Matters:** In these days of credit cards, easy loans and unbridled consumerism, most people tend to live beyond their means. In such a milieu, if you resist buying things even if you can afford them; if you live within your means, rather, below your means so that you have money for unexpected expenses, you can stand out from the crowd. In most corporates, one finds that if there is a slight delay in payment of salary, most people are upset and moan and complain because they have a lot of months left at the end of their money. If you handle your money/expenses prudently so that you have a lot of money left at the end of the month and are not upset by any delay in salary payment, you stand out. In other words, when everyone around you is struggling to make ends meet and you are not, you stand out from the crowd. You show that you are a cut above the rest.
- **Making Rational Decision:** The ninth way to stand out from the crowd is to have a rational approach to life's situations so that your responses and decisions flow out of logic and reason and are not contaminated by feelings, emotions, prejudices, pre-conceived notions and dogmas. Far too many people react emotionally to situations instead of thinking them out in a cool, calm, rational manner. Others are slaves to dogmas. They make up their minds beforehand and then "Selectively" look for facts and evidence to justify their decisions or responses and ignore or disregard those facts which support a contrary view. Such people staunchly and blindly support one party or one view or one position. Reasonable and Truth-loving persons are more balanced. They realize and accept that, in most cases, truth usually lies somewhere between the two extremes. If your views and decisions

are based on reason and logic and are made in a spirit of open-mindedness, you will stand tall and away from the majority of the people. You will stand out from the crowd.

Chapter 38

RANDOM MUSINGS AND REFLECTIONS

(*A few lessons learnt in the course of living*)

In the process of living, life has taught me some very vital lessons. Some of these are:

Happiness

I have learnt that happiness is a choice, a decision. You can be as happy as you choose to be. Happiness is an inside job. It is not what happens to you, but what happens inside you, that matters. You may not be able to control your circumstances, but you can choose your attitude, your response. Your response is entirely yours. You can be happy regardless of anything. It is wise to learn to see the 'pony' — the good — in every situation. Life is only 10 % what happens to you and 90 % how you respond.

Health

I have learnt that health is the most important. It is an unparalleled wealth. Only physical pain is real. All other pain (psychological, emotional, etc.) is self-created. It is a result of thinking. As Kathleen Casey says, "Pain is inevitable; suffering is optional."

Success

When I was unschooled in life, I equated success with fame, power, position, etc. But now I have learnt that success means peace, serenity, equanimity, equilibrium, high quality of life, harmony. A successful person is one who can fall asleep within a couple of minutes of hitting the pillow at night and can be out of the toilet within five minutes, feeling much lighter, in the morning. I have realized, as Einstein said:" The only success worth having is the freedom to live your life the way you want to". Success means being true to yourself; as a poet said, "to be nobody but yourself -in a world that is trying to make you like everybody else".

Wealth

I have learnt that the richest man in the world is not the one who has the most but the one who needs the least. In other words, contentment is the greatest wealth. When Alexander the Great told Diogenes, the poor philosopher, "Ask what you want, and I shall give it to you," the philosopher replied, "I want nothing from you but please move out of my light." Simply put, Diogenes, with no possessions, was rich because he was contented and wanted nothing. In contrast, Alexander with all the riches, the power, the fame, etc. was miserably poor because he was hungry for more.

Empathy

Empathy means understanding and sharing the feelings of another whereas sympathy is being sorry for another. For a long time, I believed that empathy means standing in the shoes of the other, of seeing things from the other's point of view.

But now I have realized that to empathize means to stand in the shoes of another with his feet, i.e. to become the other person, to really understand the person, to see his/her point of view, to feel his pain.

Being critical and judgemental

I used to be very critical and judgemental. I was always very alert and kept my eyes wide open to detect the faults and mistakes of others. But, over a period of time, I have realized that nature has given me eyes to see and eyelids not to see —to close my eyes to the faults of others. I now have a big graveyard in which I have buried the faults of my friends. I have trained myself to only see the good in others.

Being opinionated

I was very opinionated. I believed that for everything there could only be two opinions: mine and the wrong one. Today, I have learnt not to be opinionated. I am now willing to give the benefit of doubt to others. I am open to contrary positions. I have realized that no matter how thin you slice it, there are always at least two sides to every situation. I have realized that the hallmark of an educated mind is to have the ability to entertain a thought or concept without accepting or agreeing to it.

Desire to control

I had a tremendous desire to control people/events/situations. But progressively, I have realized that life unfolds itself and often you have no control whatsoever over situations/events. - I have learnt that it is prudent and wise not to try to control what is beyond your control so that you are free to control what you can.

Desire to change others

I used to have a very strong desire to change others. I spent a lot of time and energy to do so but to no avail. Sadly, I realized that the only person one can change is oneself. Here's an amusing incident of an eight-year-old boy and his parents who wanted him to eat what they thought he should eat:

The boy did not want to eat anything. In spite of repeated pleadings, the boy refused to eat what was served. In utter disgust and frustration, they yelled at him and demanded that the boy tell them what he wants to eat, because the parents strongly felt that the boy must eat something. The boy said he wanted to eat an earthworm. Bewildered and shocked, but not wanting to give up, the parents managed to fetch an earthworm and ordered the child to eat. The child cried badly and refused to eat the earthworm. When asked why, he said he wanted it fried. When the earthworm was fried, the boy continued to bawl loudly and said that the earthworm should be cut in two and that he would eat half the earthworm. Not giving up, the parents cut the earthworm as desired and pushed the plate towards the child and demanded that he eat half the worm. The boy cried more loudly and told the father, "You eat first." Frustrated and annoyed, but stoically sticking to his role, the father gathered all his willpower and swallowed half the earthworm and pushed the other half towards the child and shouted, "Eat now!" The boy cried even louder and did not touch the worm. "Now what?" screamed the father, "Why can't you eat this? You wanted this! Have it!" The boy continued to wail and said, "You ate my half; this is your half, you eat this too." Thus, in spite of their best efforts, the parents could not succeed in changing the child's behaviour.

Byzad, the great Sufi saint, narrated that when he was 20 years old, he prayed to God to grant him the power to change the world. He tried hard for 20 years but could not change the world. Becoming humbler, at the age of 40, Byzad asked God to give him the power to change only his near and dear ones — his family and friends. He tried hard for the next 20 years but could not change even a single person from amongst his friends and relatives. Totally humbled and defeated, Byzad, now 60, asked God to give him the power to change himself and lamented that he wasted 40 years of his life in trying to change others.

Affirmation and visualization

While this has been dealt with at length in another chapter, I have learnt that words have tremendous power. Self-talk is very important. Speak what you want and not what you don't want. Likewise, there is tremendous power in imagination, as Einstein said, "Imagination is more powerful than knowledge." See what you want and get what you see.

Standing out in a crowd

I have learnt that it is not necessary to be very talented and gifted to be extraordinary. If you do ordinary things in an extraordinary manner, you will stand out from the crowd. The difference between ordinary and extraordinary is only a little 'extra'.

Sense of humour

This too, is the subject of another chapter. A sense of humour is an attitude, a philosophy of life. Learn to laugh at yourself. Laugh with others, and not at others. We do not stop laughing because we grow old. We grow old because we stop laughing.

Living in the present

I used to spend a lot of time worrying about the future and regretting the past. But I have realized that the only moment we really have is the present. And yet we do not live fully in the present. I have increasingly trained myself to be in the now and value those persons and things that are present and not pine for those that are absent.

Power of giving

Over the years, I have learnt that you make a living by what you get. You make a life by what you give. Giving has tremendous power. Giving brings happiness, peace, love, a sense of empowerment, pride, accomplishment, etc.

Letting go

I realized that I had cluttered my life with too many things: with too many material possessions, worn-¬out/tired relationships, useless traditions and practices, too many `shoulds' and 'oughts', unhealthy habits, etc. I have, over the years, shed a lot of this clutter and have realized that my quality of life has improved. Less is more.

Taking life seriously

Finally, I have learnt not to take life too seriously, — anyway, I won't come out of it alive. I take my job, profession, commitments seriously, but not life. I have realized that angels fly high because they do not take themselves seriously

Suggested Reading

1. Jack Canfield — How to Get from Where you are to Where You Want to Be.
2. Esther & Jerry Hicks — Ask and It is Given.
3. Deepak Chopra — The 7 Spiritual Laws of Success.
4. Azim Jamal — The Power of Giving.
5. Shiv Khera — You can Win.
6. Carlos G.Valles — Courage to Be Myself.
7. Dale Carnegie — How to Win Friends & Influence People.
8. Dale Carnegie — Public Speaking.
9. Norman Vincent Peale — The Power of Positive Thinking.
10. Wayne Dyer—You will see it When you believe it.
11. Wayne Dyer -- The Sky's the Limit.
12. Wayne Dyer --Your Erroneous Zones.
13. Wayne Dyer --Real Magic.
14. Wayne Dyer --Your Sacred Self.
15. Napolean Hill - Think & Grow Rich.
16. Joseph Murphy — The Power of The Subconscious Mind.
17. Anthony Robbins — Awaken the Giant Within.
18. Zig Ziglar — See You at The Top.
19. Mitesh & Indu Khatri — The Law of Attraction.

About the Author

Rashid Merchant was born on 23rd October 1940. He has Master's Degrees in Economics and Law as well as a Post-Graduate Diploma in Bank Management and a Post-Graduate Diploma in Business Management. He has also successfully completed the Certificate course of All-India Institute of Bankers [C.A.I.I.B].

He worked with State Bank of India [S.B.I] for over 33 years and retired as a Senior Executive in November 2000. During his career, he was involved in various aspects of banking including Operations, Legal, Economic Research, Human Resources and Training. He retired as an Asst. General Manager & Chief Trainer in charge of S.B.I's Training Centre in Mumbai

Rashid has more than 25 years of experience conducting trainings in Personality Development, Personal Excellence, Self-Growth, Public Speaking, Effective Communication, Soft skills, etc. for Corporate Houses, NGO'S, Educational Institutes as well as the General Public. Some of his long-term training assignments were with:

- Air Hostess Academy
- The British Institute
- The Personality School

In addition to his Freelance Training Assignments, since August 2004, Rashid has been teaching in colleges (Full Time as well as Part-Time) too. As a Senior Faculty member, he has taught various subjects including Law, Business Communication, Communication Skills, Effective Personal

Transformation, Etiquette, Principles of Management, etc. at the graduate and postgraduate levels at the Anjuman College of Hotel Management and Sydenham Institute of Management studies. Currently, he is a visiting Professor at Anjuman College of Hotel Management. Additionally, Rashid also gives Motivational and Educative Talks.

Rashid is passionately fond of books and has read hundreds of books on various subjects including books on Personality Development, Self-Growth, Excellence, etc. (a small list is given on the last page of this book). In addition, Rashid has conducted and also attended numerous workshops, seminars, Training programs, etc. on these topics. This Book is born out of years of reading, thinking, participating in Workshops/ Seminars, discussing with Mentors, fellow participants in Workshops/Seminars, etc.

Rashid is extremely fond of sports and was a national level football player. He also excelled in Tennis and Badminton. He is a voracious reader and enjoys watching sports and listening to old Hindi songs.